COUNTRY

CHRISTMAS

CROSS-STITCH

COUNTRY
CHRISTMAS
CROSS-STITCH

LISBETH PERRONE

SEDGEWOOD® PRESS

For CBS, Inc.:
Editorial Director: *Dina von Zweck*
Project Coordinator: *Jacqueline Weinbach*

For Sedgewood® Press:
Editorial Director: *Elizabeth P. Rice*
Project Editor: *Lori Labriola*
Associate Editor: *Leslie Gilbert*
Production Manager: *Bill Rose*
Book Design: *Bentwood Studio/Jos. Trautwein*
Photography: *Robert Epstein*
Photo Stylist: *James Killough*

ACKNOWLEDGMENTS

To make a needle-arts book like this possible, there are always creative hands and minds involved. For making this book possible, I would like to extend my thanks and deep appreciation to my mother, Thomazine Ransjö, and Yoke van Berge Henegouwen Abolafia, Francene Garnett, June Hyne, Nora Pickens, Jacqueline Winton and Justine Chick for their help in embroidering the pieces. Also, my thanks to Sara Huntington Brown, whose skill and knowledge are obvious in the designs she charted. I would also like to thank Needle's Eye for their help in finishing the projects.

Swedish Cottage, Colonial Decorative Display Company and *The Wicker Garden* have provided many of the charming, old-fashioned accessories that we have used in photographs throughout the book. Also, *American Tree & Wreath Company* has been very kind and generous in supplying the trees and most of the other Christmas greenery. I am grateful to them for their assistance, cooperation and thoughtfulness.

And I am indebted to Dina von Zweck for her enthusiasm, ideas and professional expertise.

Santa Fe, 1985
Lisbeth

Distributed by Macmillan Publishing Company, a division of Macmillan, Inc.

ISBN 0-02-595920-4

Library of Congress Catalog Card Number: 85-50567

Printed in the United States of America.

To everyone *who* loves Christmas . . .

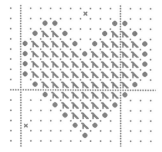

and especially to Sandy Killough,
whose generosity of spirit and superb
decorating skills helped make
this book possible.

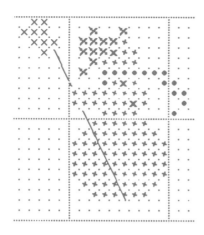

CONTENTS

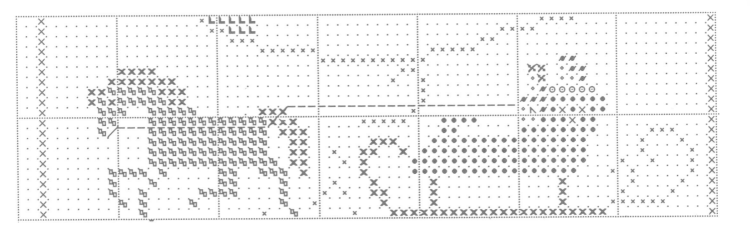

INTRODUCTION

An old-fashioned, country Christmas is the traditional notion of what the season is all about—the sweet cinnamon smell of cookies baking in the oven, a freshly-cut tree trimmed with gold ornaments and red plaid ribbons, and a house filled with cheerful decorations. This year, add the joy of Christmas cross-stitch to your plans for the holiday season. A beautiful handmade wall hanging or personalized Christmas stocking will bring you a sense of great satisfaction. Creating exquisite handiwork is an enriching and worthwhile pastime, and you will enjoy your finished pieces for years and years to come. They also make wonderful gifts for family and friends. Wouldn't you love making an ornament for baby's first Christmas? Or the Dancing Gnomes Pillow for Aunt Betty?

This book was produced with you in mind. The designs are very special . . . and they're meant to give you hours and hours of creative pleasure. The finished projects are ones that you will be proud and happy to display in your home . . . or give as gifts. All the cross-stitch pieces are a happy blend of bright colors and imaginative motifs. I hope they will bring the peaceful Christmas spirit into your whole life. It has been a joyous book to make, and I hope you will find many projects that will enrich your holiday.

GENERAL INSTRUCTIONS

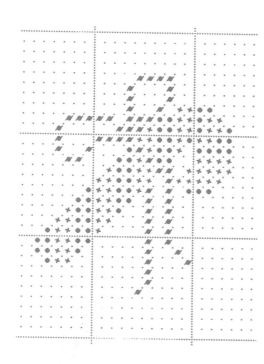

HOW TO USE AND WORK WITH THIS BOOK

Each design in COUNTRY CHRISTMAS CROSS-STITCH is worked in cross-stitch embroidery and is shown in full color. And each design has its own work-chart done in symbols. Each symbol represents one stitch in a particular color. The symbols are carried through the same way on all charts. (For example, the symbol for red will be the same throughout the book.) A change in symbol on a chart means a change of color. The grid of the work-chart represents your material. It is the background of your finished piece. Each square on the grid represents the area for one stitch. Blank squares in the charts represent areas left unstitched. If a chart extends over more than one page, the grid will indicate how and where to continue onto the next work-chart.

To make any of the motifs in the book, you need only to know two stitches: the cross-stitch and the backstitch. This book can be used by the beginner, the intermediate or advanced embroiderer. You can follow our designs and color combinations, or you can change the colors and rearrange the designs, and make your own additions. Remember, this is a workbook that you can use exactly as is or, if you are experienced in cross-stitch, you can rearrange the motifs to create your own designs.

Throughout the book, we have used DMC cotton embroidery floss. We have given the actual color number next to each symbol. If you cannot find the exact number in your local needlework store, a number close to the one we used will be fine, since the color range is very wide. You can, of course, use any thread you like, as long as it is suitable for your background material. A good rule to remember is to pick a thread that is equally as thick or thin as the warp and weft thread in the fabric. When I estimate the amount of thread needed for a project, I figure approximately one yard of thread per square inch.

For each project we have also specified which kind of material we used, and how many strands of floss are recommended for good coverage. Of course, you can choose a different background material; just make sure that the appropriate thread is picked for the size fabric used.

We did most of our embroideries on even-weave linen #18. Personally, I like to work on an attractive even-weave linen, since the background in cross-stitch is usually left unstitched. Linens have a lovely sheen, and they get more and more attractive over the years. Cross-stitch has become very popular over the last few years, so you will find that needlework stores throughout the country are now carrying a large assortment of even-weave fabrics.

For some of the projects, where stated, we used Aida cloth #12 and #14.

The cutting size and actual finished size is also given for each project.

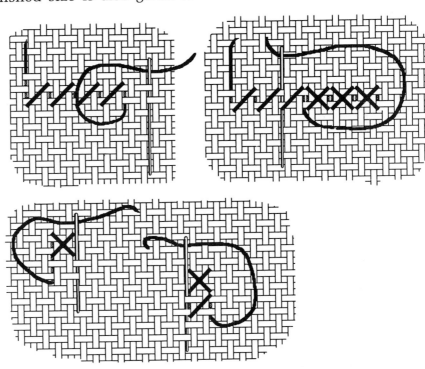

THE STITCHES

Cross-Stitch
This stitch is also known as the sampler stitch. It is worked on an even-weave material on which the threads can be counted. The crosses should be of an even shape, and the top stitches should always slant in the same direction.

Backstitch
The backstitch is used to highlight and connect a shape or figure done in cross-stitch. It can be worked in all directions. The stitch covers two threads on the even-weave linens, and one square on the Aida cloth.

See diagrams for a clearer understanding of how to do these stitches.

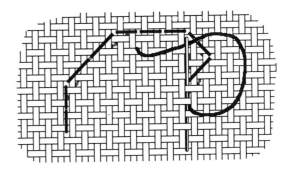

TOOLS AND MATERIALS

Embroidery Basket
Keep all your tools and materials in one place. An easily accessible and portable basket will hold everything you need, and give you a sense of organization.

Needles
The needle is the oldest tool of decorative expression. Needles used for cross-stitch should have a blunt end. The higher the number on the package, the finer the needles. We used #22 and #24 for the projects in the book. Always keep a few extra needles in your basket. Somehow, they tend to vanish!

Scissors
Keep two sets in your basket. A heavier pair for cutting the materials; and a finer pair for the threads.

Thimble
If you are used to working with a thimble, choose one that is deep and fairly rounded.

Marker
Keep a water-soluble marker in your basket for indicating lines and marking the center.

Push Pins
These will come in handy for blocking and stretching. Make sure that they are rustproof.

Hoop or Frame
A hoop or frame is usually not necessary for cross-stitch. However, if you feel more comfortable working with one, keep a few different sizes in your basket.

Notebook
A small notebook and pencil will come in handy for jotting down ideas—otherwise, they may be forgotten!

Even-weave Materials
Even-weaves come in different widths and sizes. The coarseness, or fineness, of the material is measured by the number of stitches per inch. The lower the number of the size, the coarser the material. For the book we have used #18 even-weave linen, and #12 and #14 Aida cloth. On the #18 even-weave linen, you will get 9 stitches per inch, since you are covering two threads in each direction for one stitch. On the Aida cloth, however, the background is woven in squares, each stitch covering one square. Keep this in mind, since a #18 even-weave will only give you 9 stitches per inch, and the #18 Aida cloth will give you 18 stitches per inch— a 100% difference in the size. Until you become really familiar with the different types of even-weaves, consult your local needlework store as to sizes and types of materials needed for your projects.

Remember, there is a difference between even-weave *linens* and even-weave *squared fabrics*.

Threads
As mentioned, throughout the book we have used the 6-strand DMC embroidery floss. The advantage of this thread is that it is readily available, and easily separated. We have indicated how many strands were used for each project (in terms of background material for that project). Should you choose a different thread or different size fabric, be sure that you get the right combination of both. The thread should flow easily in and out of the material and give your stitches good coverage. As you become more experienced as an embroiderer, you will quickly learn what works best. If you feel uncertain, check with your local needlework store.

HOW TO START A PROJECT, FOLLOW A CHART AND FINISH YOUR WORK

Select your project, and then purchase the necessary material and threads. Do not compromise when it comes to quality. The best quality will give the best results. You can use the same materials and threads that we have used, or you may choose different types. If so, make sure that the combination is correct. Consult your local needlework store if you feel at all uncertain. Allow enough material for finishing your piece. I always allow a good 2″ all around, unless it is a very small project. Then prepare your material by "whipstitching" around the edges with regular sewing thread. (To whipstitch, insert a threaded sewing needle at a right angle to the fabric edge. Make overcast stitches over the edge, spacing them evenly, at a uniform depth. The resulting slanted stitches will keep the edges from fraying.)

Find the center of your material by folding it in half: first horizontally, then vertically. Where the folds intersect, mark the center with a water-soluble pen. Now find the center of the work-chart. That is where you should start to work.

Follow the chart carefully. Also, keep the following hints in mind. Never knot your thread. Fasten and secure by weaving it in and out on the back of the material. The threads should be secured in the same direction as the stitches; otherwise, they may show through. Do not pull the thread too tightly, just as you shouldn't leave it too loose. Keep an even rhythm. The thread you are working with should be no longer than 18 inches. If the thread gets twisted, hold the fabric up, and let the threaded needle hang down. It will unwind the same as a telephone cord.

When you have finished the actual embroidery, it is time to check your work carefully. Hold your work up to the light, and you will discover if there are any missing stitches. If so, fill them in. Check and make sure that all ends are securely fastened on the back. Clip and trim unnecessarily long threads on the back.

Cross-stitch done on even-weave materials should not have to be blocked. If you see that your work is pulling out of shape while embroidering, stop and correct the problem. You are probably working with a thread that is too heavy, so the combination between the thread and fabric is incorrect.

A good pressing should be enough to prepare the piece for finishing. Lay the piece face down, and press with a damp cloth. Repeat if necessary. Should the piece need cleaning, dip it in a mild soap solution, then press with a dry cloth. For mounting and framing the work yourself, consult one of the many books available on the subject. Also, most needlework stores carry a wide variety of articles and inserts.

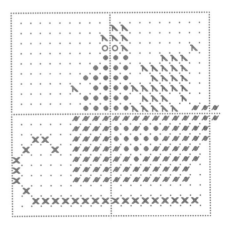

TREE TRIMMINGS

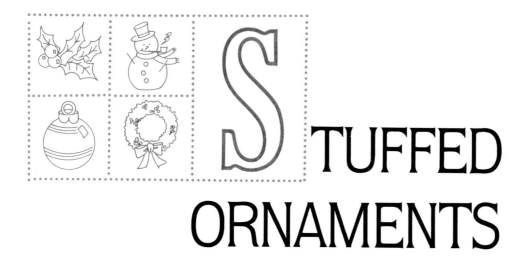

STUFFED ORNAMENTS

● Plump, stuffed ornaments will add extra cheer to a traditional tree decorated with Christmas balls and ribbon. We backed ours with the same material as the front, and stuffed them with fiberfill—then whipstitched the edges with gold cording. A bow and loop decorate the top of each ornament.

STUFFED ORNAMENTS

Cut size: 6″ × 6″
Finished size: approximately 2″ × 2″ overall

#12 Aida cloth
  3 strands of floss

        OR

#18 even-weave linen
  4 strands of floss

Use metallic thread wherever indicated.

GIFT PACKAGE

	DMC#	
• • • • •	349	red
ʟ ʟ ʟ ʟ ʟ	989	med. olive
◣ ◣ ◣ ◣ ◣	3346	dk. olive

SLED

	DMC#	
• • • • •	349	red
◢ ◢ ◢ ◢ ◢	321	scarlet
ο ο ο ο ο	819	pink
ʌ ʌ ʌ ʌ ʌ	701	med. green
x x x x x	823	deep ultramarine blue

NOEL

	DMC#	
• • • • •	349	red
x x x x x	725	gold
ʌ ʌ ʌ ʌ ʌ	701	med. green

LAMB

	DMC#	
x x x x x	433	chocolate
+ + + + +		white

BIRD

	DMC#	
• • • • •	349	red
⁄ ⁄ ⁄ ⁄ ⁄	307	lt. yellow
◂ ◂ ◂ ◂ ◂	318	med. grey
ʌ ʌ ʌ ʌ ʌ	701	med. green
v v v v v	907	chartreuse
x x x x x	823	deep ultramarine blue
+ + + + +		white

GOLD-WINGED ANGEL

	DMC#	
ο ο ο ο ο	819	pink
x x x x x	725	gold
▪ ▪ ▪ ▪ ▪	824	dk. blue
÷ ÷ ÷ ÷ ÷		gold metallic
————	823	deep ultramarine blue backstitch

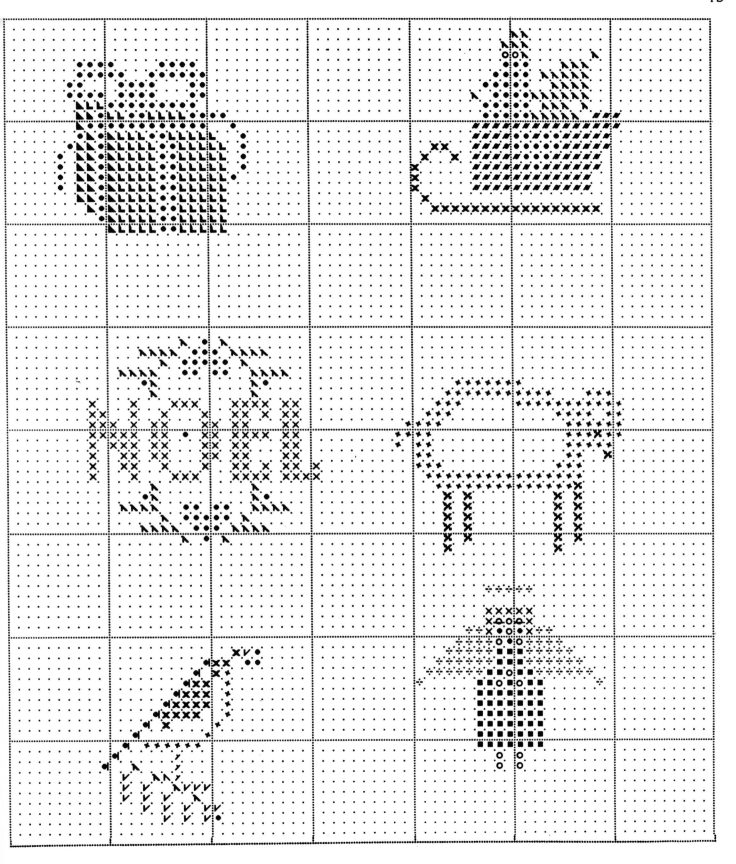

20

CHRISTMAS TREE

DMC#

• • • • •	349	red
↳↳↳↳↳	400	chestnut
ʌʌʌʌʌ	701	med. green
÷÷÷÷÷		gold metallic

ANGEL AND CANDLE

DMC#

• • • • •	349	red
⊙⊙⊙⊙⊙	602	dk. pink
○○○○○	819	pink
✗✗✗✗✗	433	chocolate
✗✗✗✗✗	725	gold
ɹɹɹɹɹ	307	lt. yellow
x x x x x		silver metallic
——————	823	deep ultramarine blue backstitch

CANDY CANE

DMC#

• • • • •	349	red
✗✗✗✗✗	321	scarlet
✦✦✦✦✦		white

SNOWMAN

DMC#

• • • • •	349	red
✗✗✗✗✗	725	gold
✗✗✗✗✗	433	chocolate
✗✗✗✗✗	823	deep ultramarine blue
——————	823	deep ultramarine blue backstitch

APPLE

DMC#

• • • • •	349	red
x x x x x		silver metallic
ʌʌʌʌʌ	701	med. green

BELL

DMC#

• • • • •	349	red
✗✗✗✗✗	725	gold
ʌʌʌʌʌ	701	med. green
÷÷÷÷÷		gold metallic

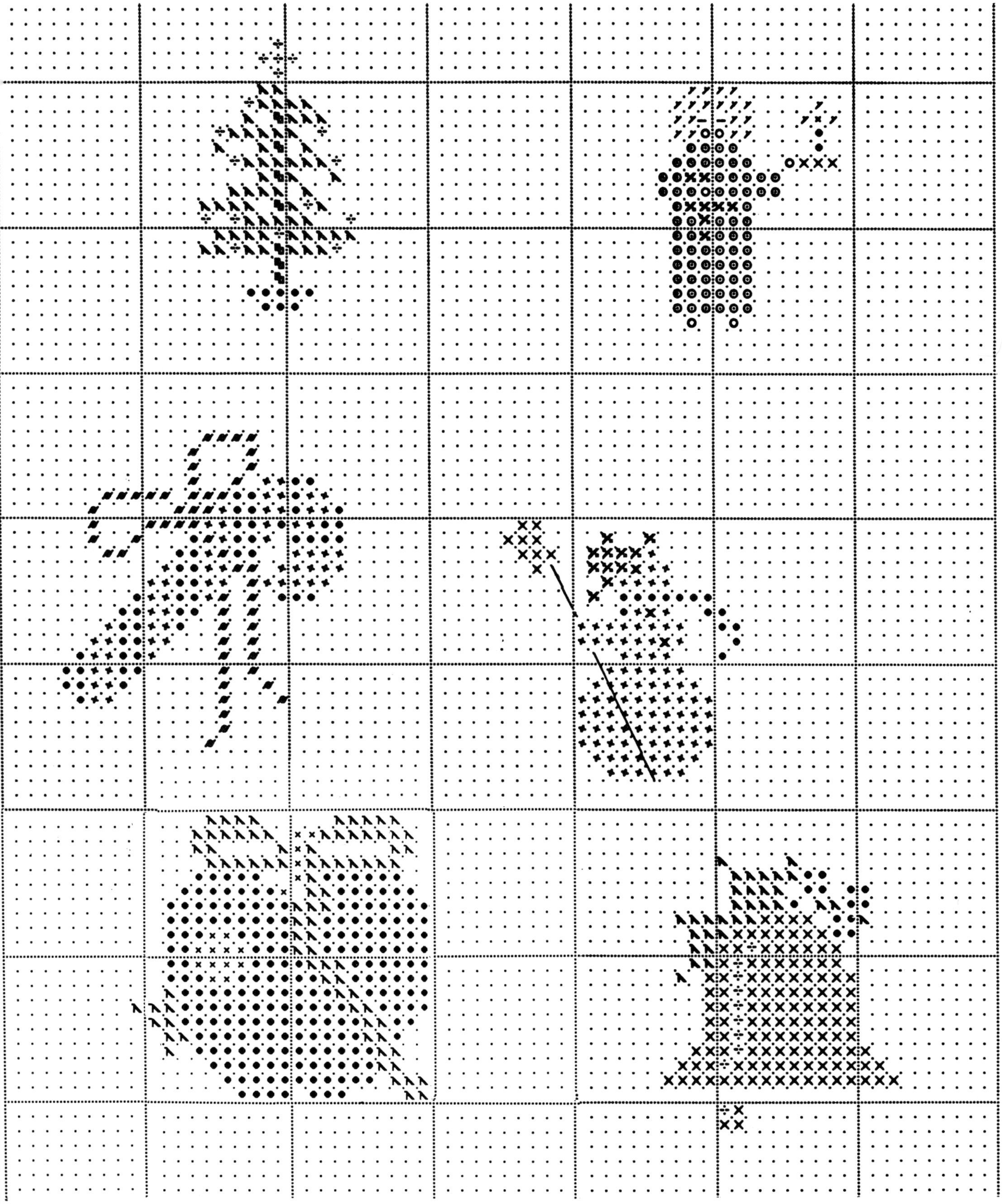

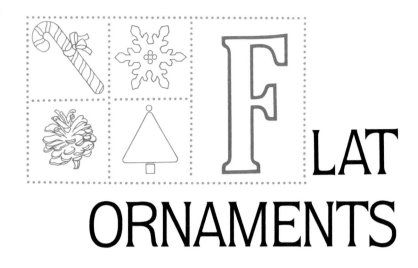

FLAT ORNAMENTS

● *These framed ornaments will give your tree a delightful country Christmas look. Most needlework stores throughout the country carry a wide assortment of frames for ornaments. Simple, as well as attractive, framed ornaments are fun to embroider as gifts.*

In addition to the ornaments that we have shown, you can pick up motifs from other projects in the book, and create your own ornaments. The initials of a friend or family member would make an attractive Christmas ornament.

FLAT ORNAMENTS

Cut size: 6″ × 6″
Finished size: approximately 2″ × 2″ overall

#12 Aida cloth
  3 strands of floss

        OR

#18 even-weave linen
  4 strands of floss

Use metallic thread wherever indicated.

HEART

	DMC#	
• • • • •	349	red
✗ ✗ ✗ ✗ ✗	321	scarlet
⋀ ⋀ ⋀ ⋀ ⋀	701	med. green

MOUSE

	DMC#	
• • • • •	349	red
o o o o o	819	pink
✗ ✗ ✗ ✗ ✗	725	gold
۹ ۹ ۹ ۹ ۹	415	dove grey
✦ ✦ ✦ ✦ ✦		white

HOLLY

	DMC#	
• • • • •	349	red
✗ ✗ ✗ ✗ ✗	321	scarlet
⋀ ⋀ ⋀ ⋀ ⋀	701	med. green
⋀ ⋀ ⋀ ⋀ ⋀	3346	dk. olive

GIFT BASKET

	DMC#	
• • • • •	349	red
✗ ✗ ✗ ✗ ✗	321	scarlet
⋎ ⋎ ⋎ ⋎ ⋎	307	lt. yellow
⋎ ⋎ ⋎ ⋎ ⋎	782	bronze
✗ ✗ ✗ ✗ ✗	725	gold
⋀ ⋀ ⋀ ⋀ ⋀	701	med. green
✦ ✦ ✦ ✦ ✦		white

CANDLE

	DMC#	
• • • • •	349	red
✗ ✗ ✗ ✗ ✗	321	scarlet
⋎ ⋎ ⋎ ⋎ ⋎	307	lt. yellow
⋀ ⋀ ⋀ ⋀ ⋀	701	med. green
✧ ✧ ✧ ✧ ✧		gold metallic

CARDINAL BIRD

	DMC#	
• • • • •	349	red
✗ ✗ ✗ ✗ ✗	321	scarlet
⋎ ⋎ ⋎ ⋎ ⋎	973	med. yellow
⋀ ⋀ ⋀ ⋀ ⋀	701	med. green
✗ ✗ ✗ ✗ ✗	823	deep ultramarine blue

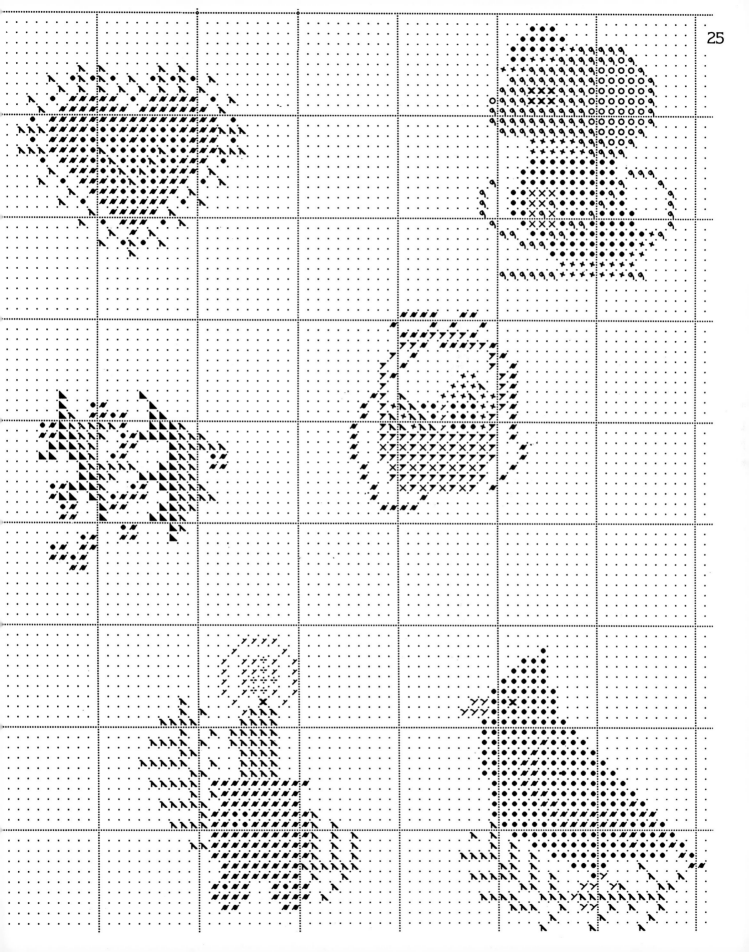

PINE CONES

	DMC#	
● ● ● ● ●	349	red
ъ ъ ъ ъ ъ	400	chestnut
ʏ ʏ ʏ ʏ ʏ	782	bronze
ʌ ʌ ʌ ʌ ʌ	701	med. green
x x x x x	823	deep ultramarine blue

PIG

	DMC#	
● ● ● ● ●	349	red
◢ ◢ ◢ ◢ ◢	321	scarlet
o o o o o	819	pink
ʏ ʏ ʏ ʏ ʏ	973	med. yellow
▲ ▲ ▲ ▲ ▲	3346	dk. olive
ʌ ʌ ʌ ʌ ʌ	701	med. green
x x x x x	823	deep ultramarine blue

GNOME

	DMC#	
● ● ● ● ●	349	red
◢ ◢ ◢ ◢ ◢	321	scarlet
. . . . .	948	flesh
ʏ ʏ ʏ ʏ ʏ	782	bronze
▽ ▽ ▽ ▽ ▽	783	gold ochre
ʌ ʌ ʌ ʌ ʌ	701	med. green
▲ ▲ ▲ ▲ ▲	3346	dk. olive
x x x x x	823	deep ultramarine blue
+ + + + +		white

TEDDY BEAR

	DMC#	
● ● ● ● ●	349	red
o o o o o	819	pink
ʏ ʏ ʏ ʏ ʏ	782	bronze
x x x x x	433	chocolate
x x x x x	823	deep ultramarine blue

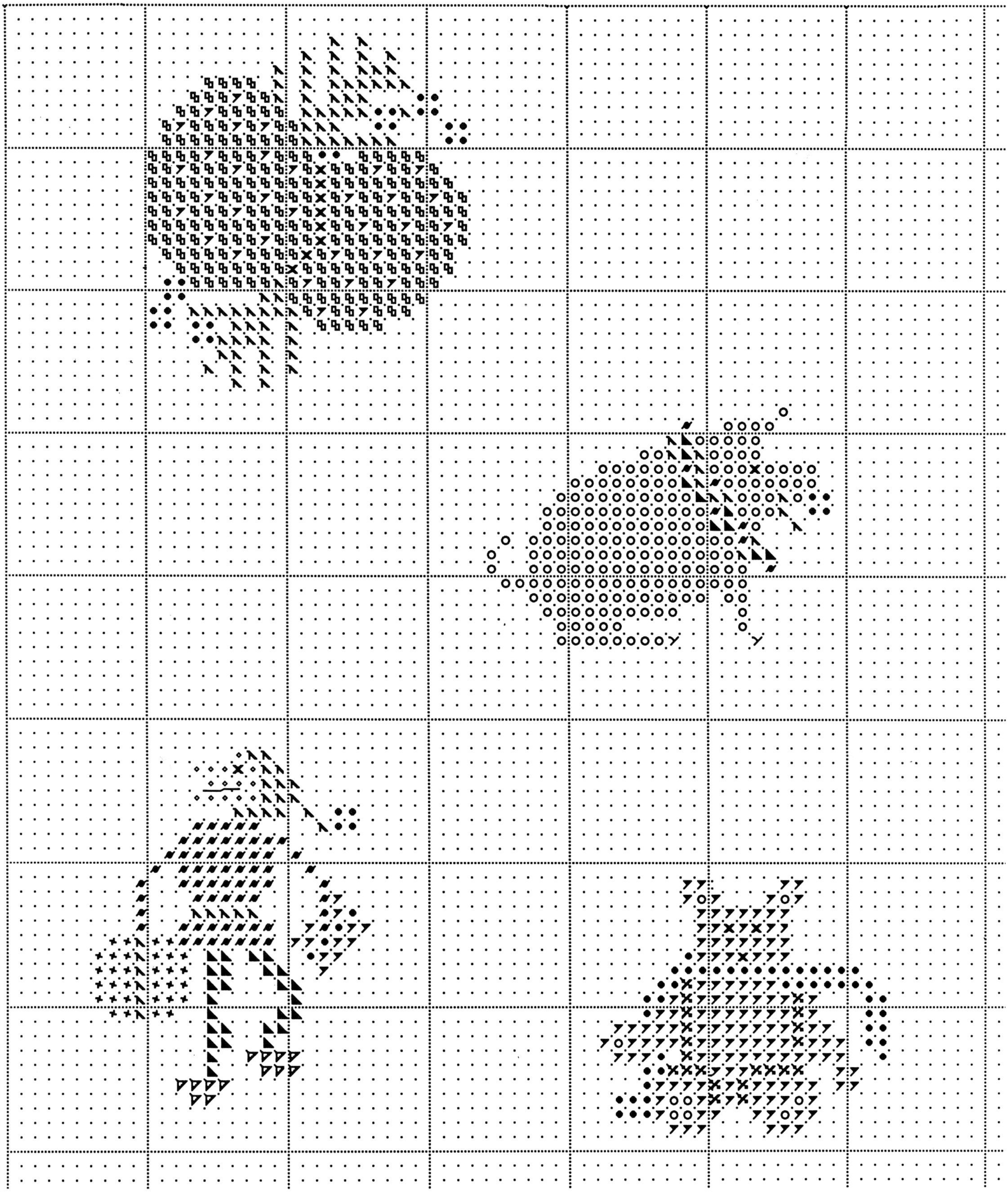

ROCKING HORSE

	DMC#	
• • • • •	349	red
✔✔✔✔✔	321	scarlet
⊙⊙⊙⊙⊙	602	dk. pink
✗✗✗✗✗	823	deep ultramarine blue
◄◄◄◄◄	318	med. grey

JOLLY SANTA

	DMC#	
• • • • •	349	red
✔✔✔✔✔	321	scarlet
• • • • •	948	flesh
✔✔✔✔✔	307	lt. yellow
+ + + + +		white
✗✗✗✗✗	823	deep ultramarine blue
‿‿‿	823	deep ultramarine blue backstitch

DOVE

	DMC#	
• • • • •	349	red
⊙⊙⊙⊙⊙	602	dk. pink
ʟʟʟʟʟ	989	med. olive
+ + + + +		white

DANCING GNOME

	DMC#	
• • • • •	349	red
✔✔✔✔✔	321	scarlet
• • • • •	948	flesh
կկկկկ	400	chestnut
ʌʌʌʌʌ	701	med. green
✗✗✗✗✗	823	deep ultramarine blue

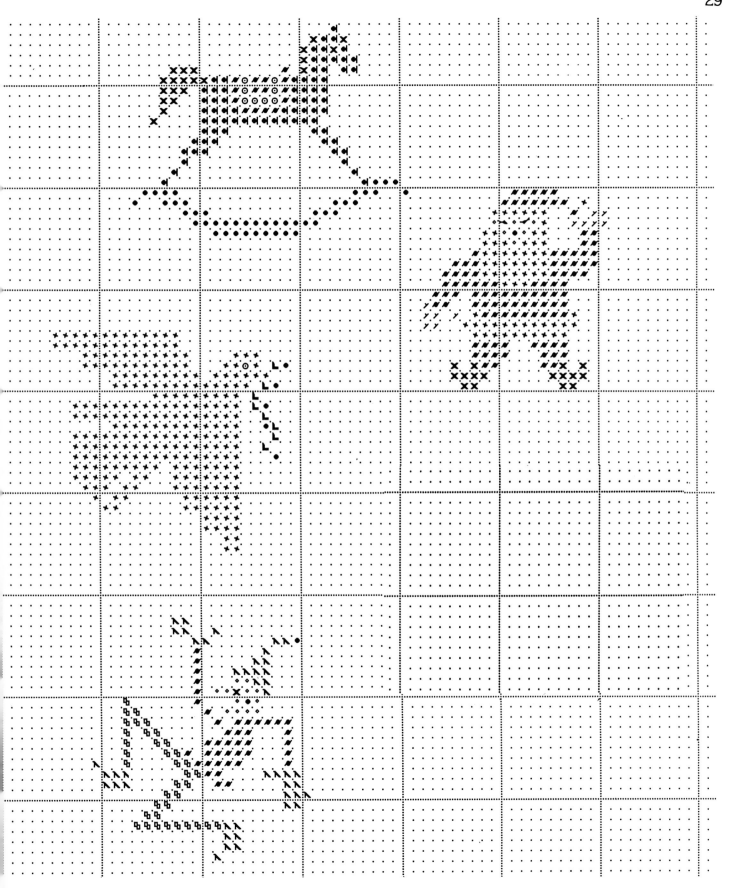

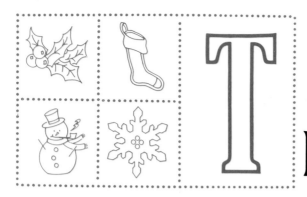 REE SKIRTS

TREES AND HEARTS TREE SKIRT

• *A tree is not really fully "dressed" without a tree skirt. The bright flounces and happy hearts add a festive background to piles of gaily-wrapped packages—and the tree skirt protects your rug and floor.*

The trees on the skirt can all be filled in with cross-stitch, or they can be outlined; we did both.

The ruffle is usually sewn on after the embroidery is finished. Most fabric stores carry a variety of colorful ruffles by-the-yard.

TREES AND HEARTS TREE SKIRT

Cut size: 44″ diameter
Finished size: 40″ diameter

#12 Aida cloth, white
  4 strands of floss
  4 yd. ruffle

      DMC#
⊖⊖⊖⊖⊖ 349 red
ʌʌʌʌʌʌ 701 med. green

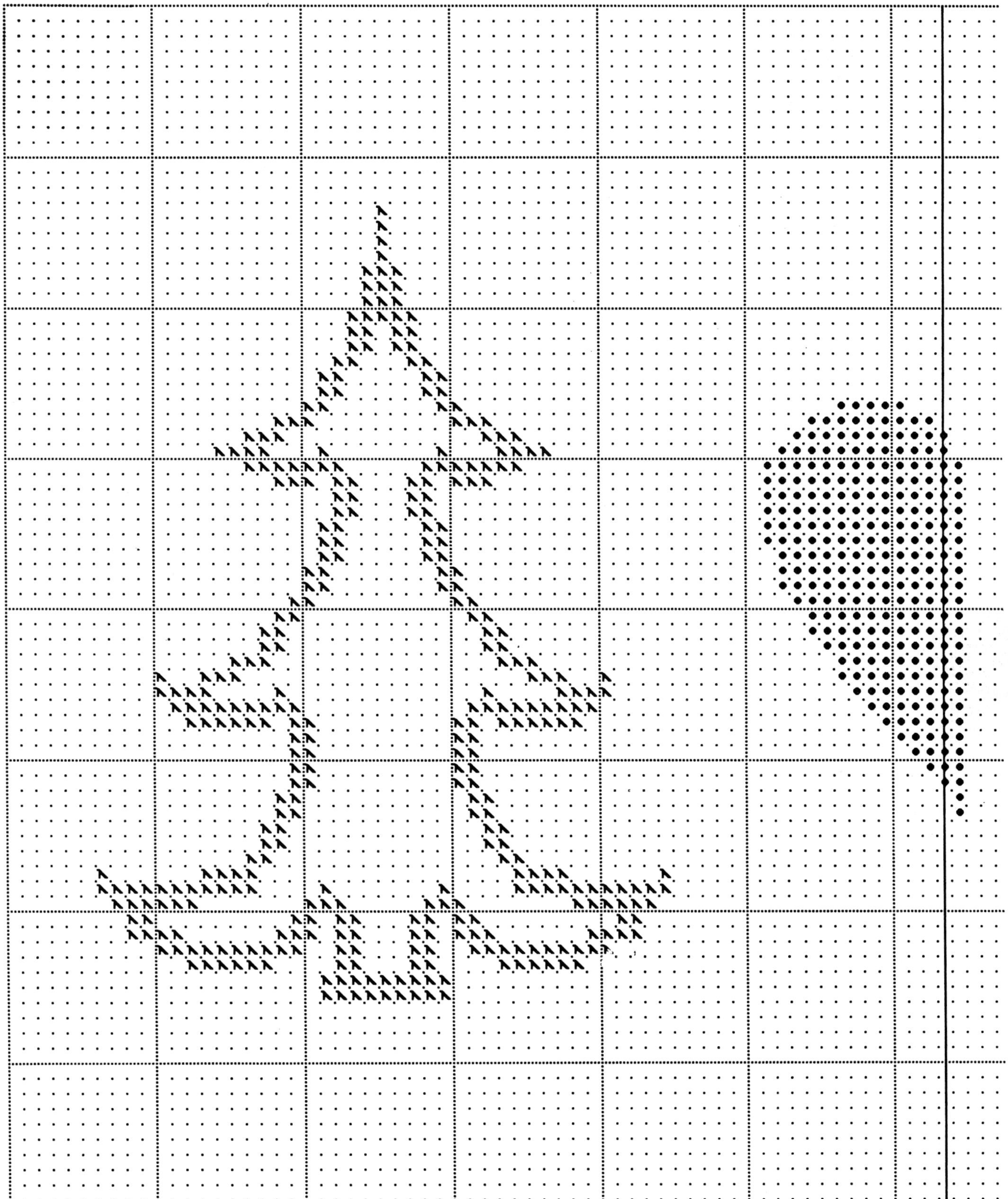

CHRISTMAS PIG TREE SKIRT

● *This silly circle of dancing pigs will make anyone smile. You can cross-stitch the entire pig, or you can outline it (the way we did). This design is quick and easy to make. You can also embroider one pig, and make a pillow or small hanging.*

This tree skirt is tailored differently from the Trees and Hearts Tree Skirt: this one opens like a cape. After you have cut the material into a circular shape, cut out a center hole (approximately 8″ diameter), then slit the material from one edge to the hole. This tailoring makes it easier to place the tree skirt around the tree.

CHRISTMAS PIG TREE SKIRT

Cut size: 44″ diameter
Finished size: 40″ diameter

#12 Aida cloth
  4 strands of floss
  6 yd. ruffle

                 DMC#
● ● ● ● ● 3687 dusty rose
———— 823   deep ultramarine
                blue

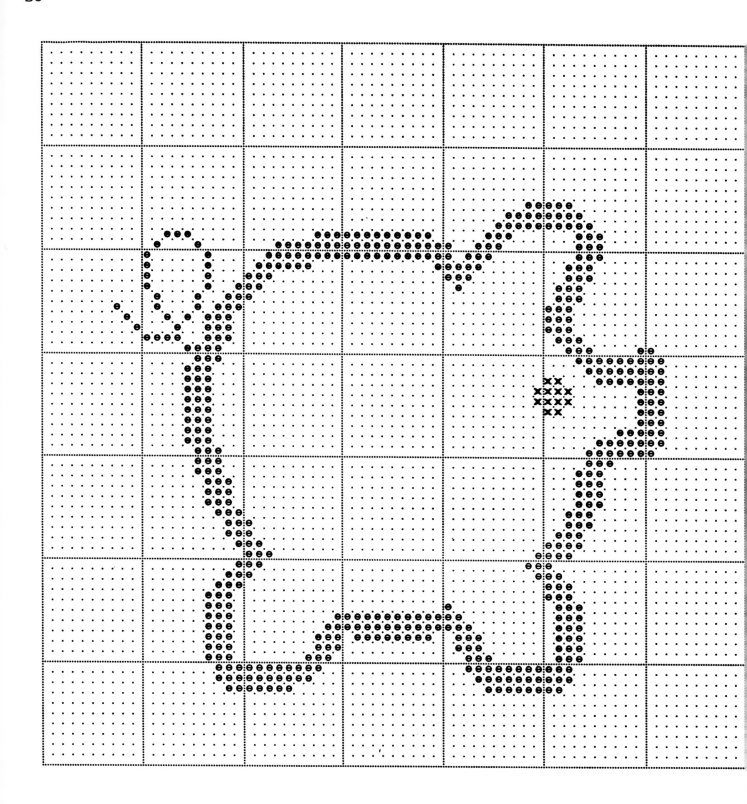

STOCKINGS

HEARTS AND PINE CONES STOCKING

● *Hearts, pine cones, candles, balls and a curious mouse. A Christmas brimming with anticipation.*

This stocking looks more complicated and time-consuming than it is. All shapes are repeated. That means that once you have cross-stitched one pine cone, all other pine cones are identical.

HEARTS AND PINE CONES STOCKIN

Cut size: 20″ × 14″
Finished size: 14″ long;
8″ wide at top

#12 Aida cloth
  3 strands of floss
  4 yd. gold metallic thread
  1 yd. silver metallic thread

	DMC#	
● ● ● ●	349	red
o o o o o	819	pink
⸜ ⸜ ⸜ ⸜	307	lt. yellow
ƌ ƌ ƌ ƌ ƌ	434	coffee
⸝⸝⸝⸝⸝	436	cafe au lait
∧∧∧∧∧	701	med. green
◁◁◁◁◁	318	med. grey
⅂⅂⅂⅂⅂	413	charcoal grey
x x x x x		silver metallic
˙˙˙˙˙˙˙˙˙		gold metallic backstitch
....	413	charcoal grey backstitch

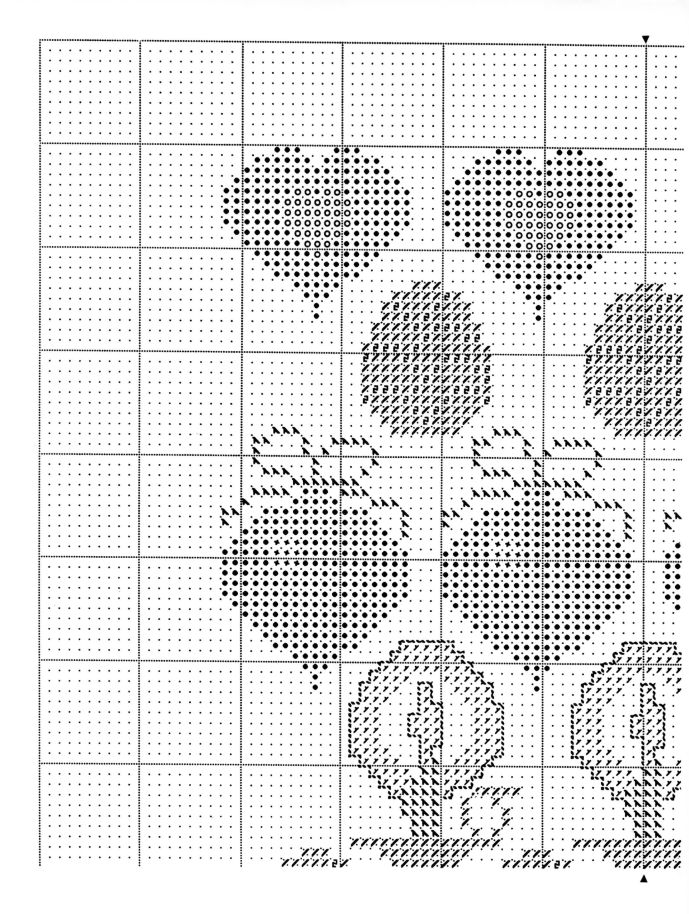

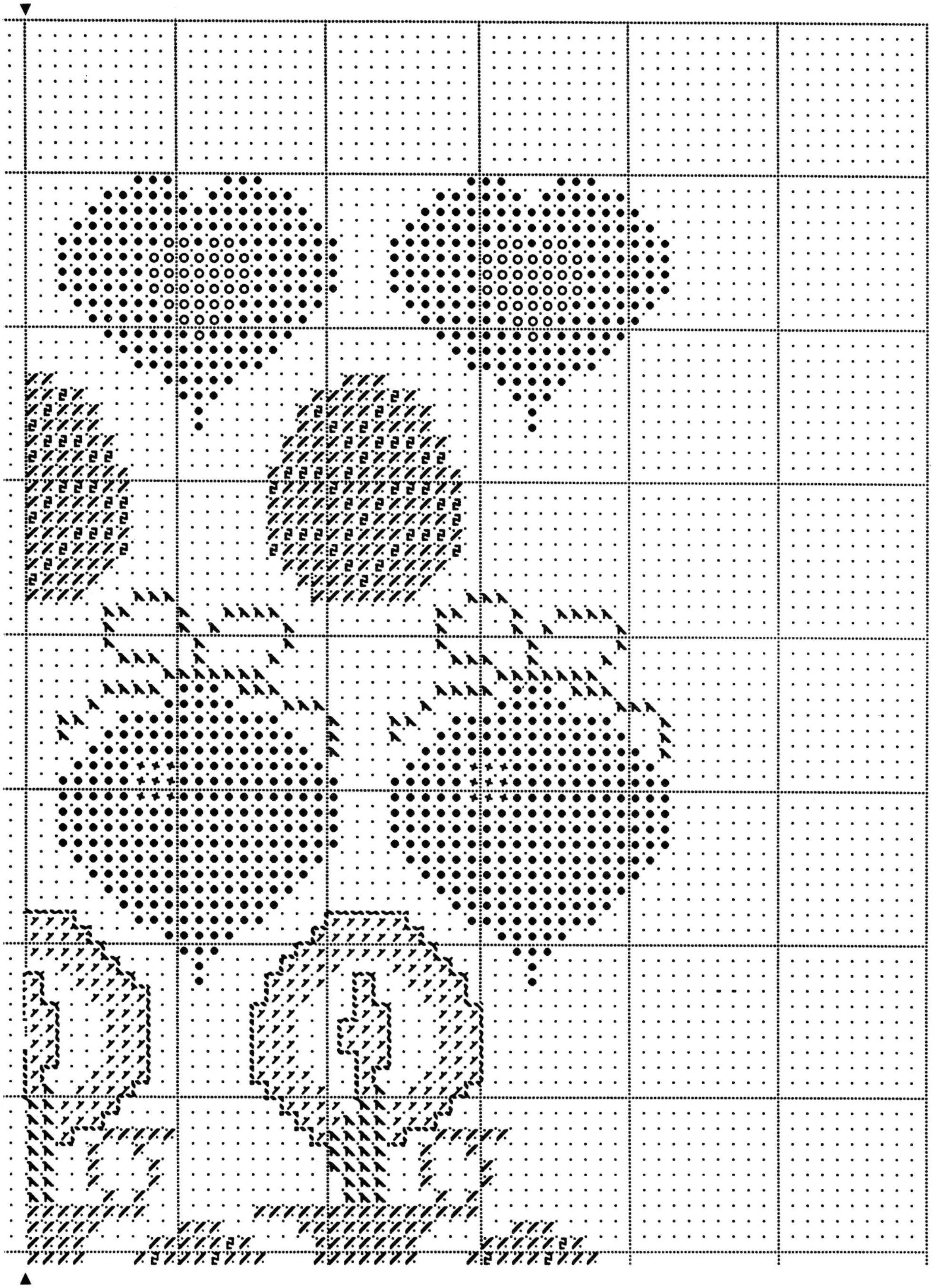

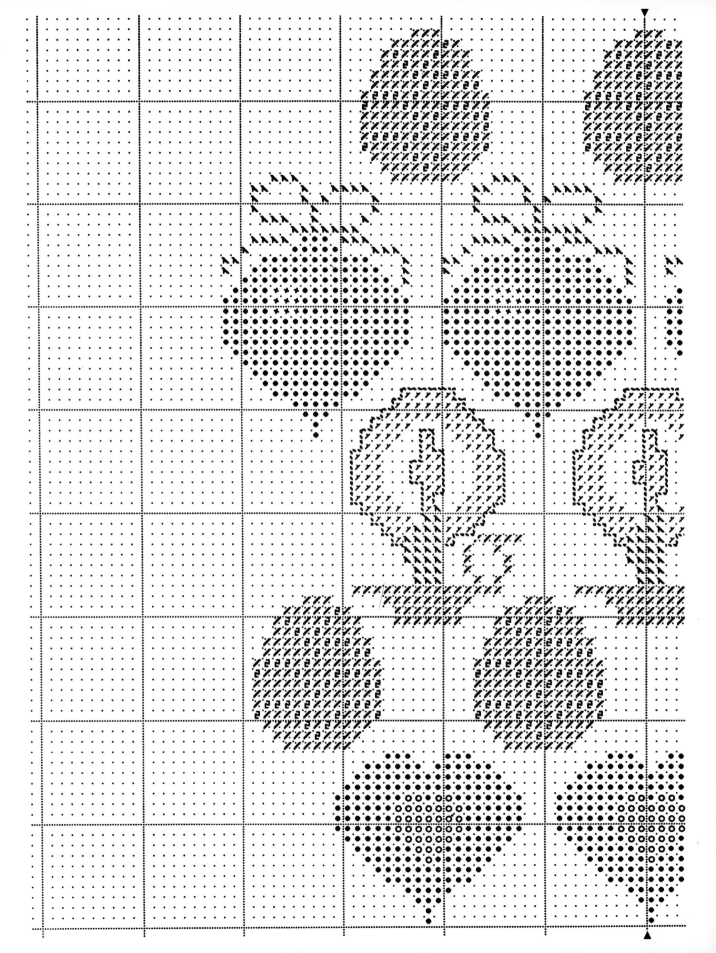

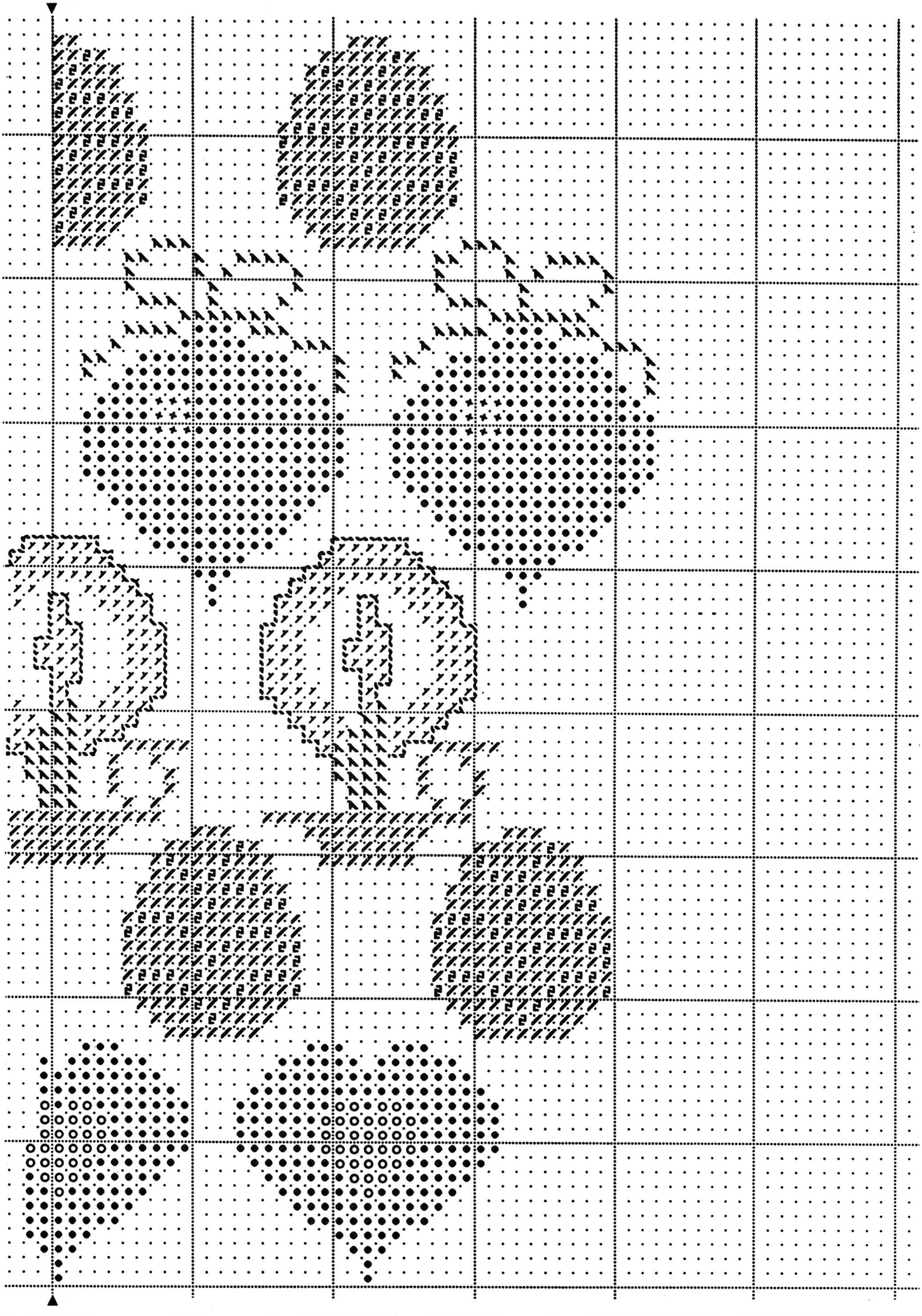

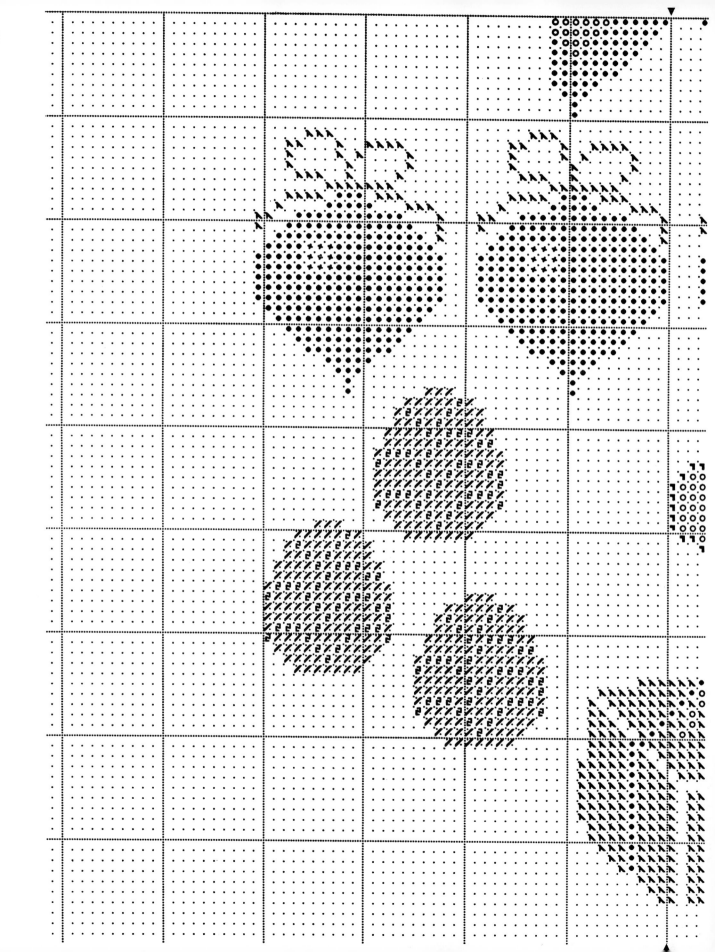

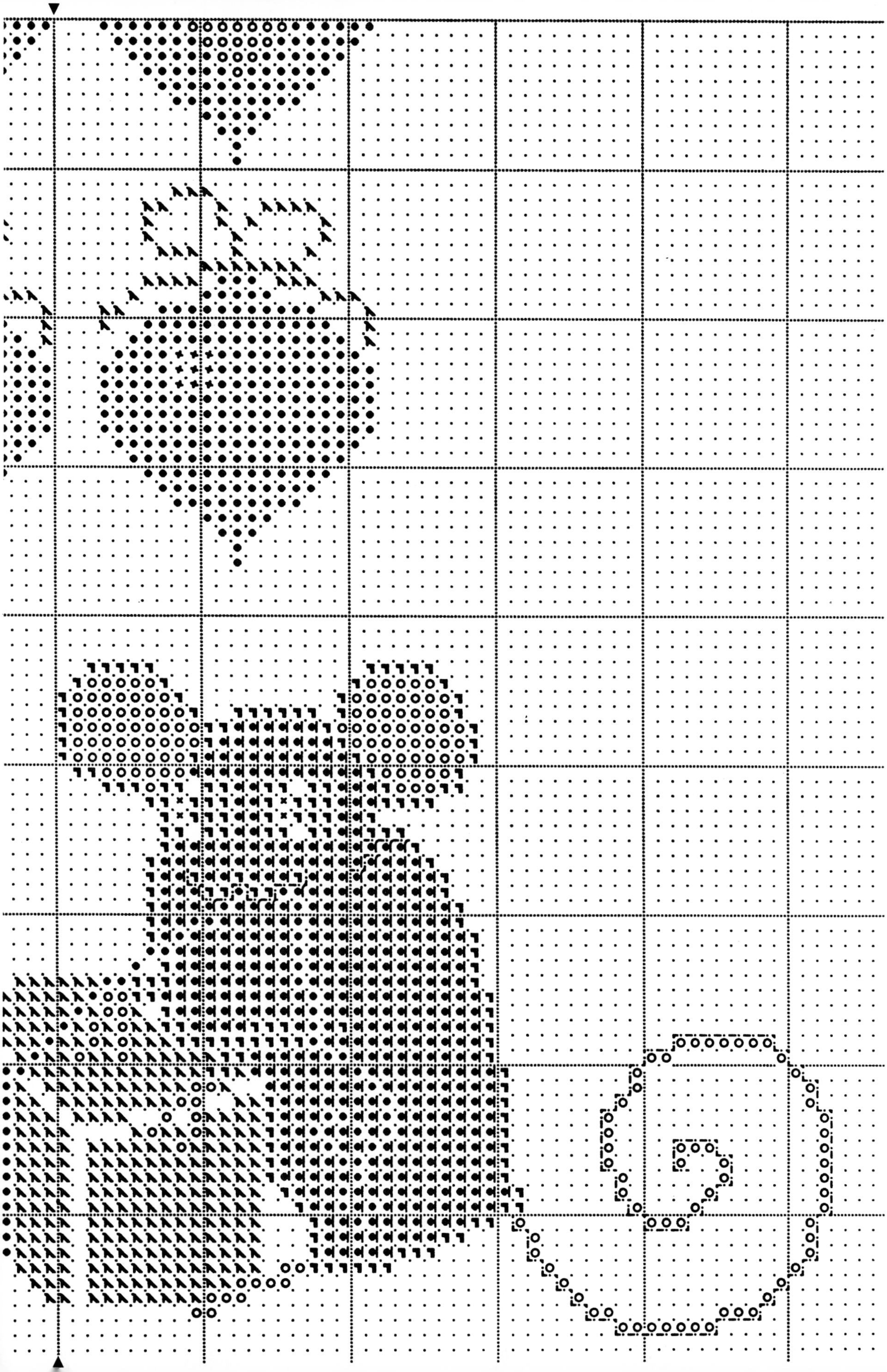

SANTA AND PRESENTS STOCKING

● *Santa with a sackful of goodies! The gifts are bountiful . . . and so are the colors. But keep in mind that the many colors used in this design will make the project somewhat ambitious. If you like, you can simplify the piece by eliminating some colors.*

SANTA AND PRESENTS STOCKING

Cut size: 20″ × 14″
Finished size: 14″ long;
8″ wide at top.

#18 even-weave linen
   4 strands of floss
   4 yd. silver metallic thread

	DMC#			DMC#	
••••••	349	red	ʌʌʌʌʌʌ	701	med. green
⊕⊕⊕⊕⊕⊕	3687	dusty rose	vvvvvv	907	chartreuse
oooooo	819	pink	＼＼＼＼＼＼	955	lt. emerald
◇◇◇◇◇◇	948	flesh	□□□□□□	799	med. blue
øøøøøø	947	orange	■■■■■■	824	dk. blue
ʏʏʏʏʏʏ	973	med. yellow	♠♠♠♠♠♠	598	aquamarine
ɤɤɤɤɤɤ	782	bronze	◊◊◊◊◊◊	208	lilac
xxxxxx	433	chocolate	⊡⊡⊡⊡⊡⊡	550	dk. purple
xxxxx	823	deep ultramarine blue	⊞⊞⊞⊞⊞⊞	718	med. red violet
۹۹۹۹۹۹	415	dove grey	＋＋＋＋＋＋		white
			x x x x x		silver metallic
			⌒‿	823	deep ultramarine blue backstitch connected

48

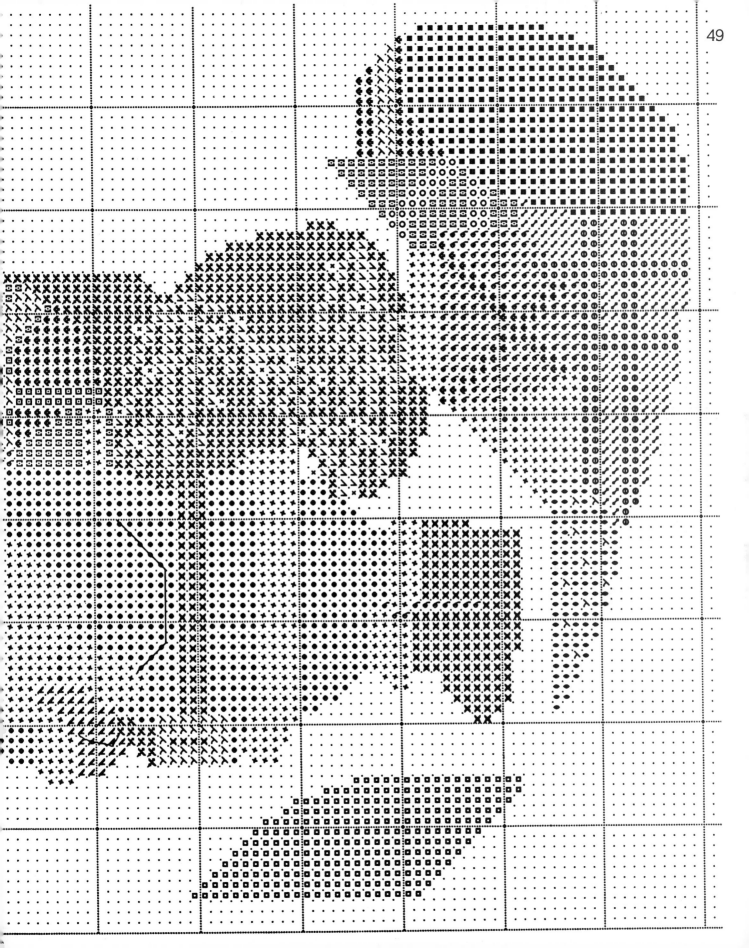

CHRISTMAS TEDDY BEAR STOCKING

● There is always room for a teddy bear in your life. And what better place than on a Christmas stocking? The bear can be personalized (see Alphabet page 187), or you can cross-stitch a name or date into the big, yellow heart. The background is filled with silver stars. These can be placed at random, or you can use the chart, and place them as we did.

This design is easy to make, because it has simple and direct shapes.

CHRISTMAS TEDDY BEAR STOCKING

Cut size: 20″ × 14″
Finished size: 14″ long;
             8″ wide at top.

#18 even-weave linen
  4 strands of floss
  4 yd. silver metallic thread

	DMC#	
● ● ● ● ●	349	red
○ ○ ○ ○ ○	894	lt. strawberry
ʏ ʏ ʏ ʏ ʏ	973	med. yellow
ƨ ƨ ƨ ƨ ƨ	434	coffee
╱ ╱ ╱ ╱ ╱	842	tan
ʌ ʌ ʌ ʌ ʌ	701	med. green
■ ■ ■ ■ ■	824	dk. blue
✕ ✕ ✕ ✕ ✕	823	deep ultramarine blue
✦ ✦ ✦ ✦ ✦		white
✕ ✕ ✕ ✕		silver metallic

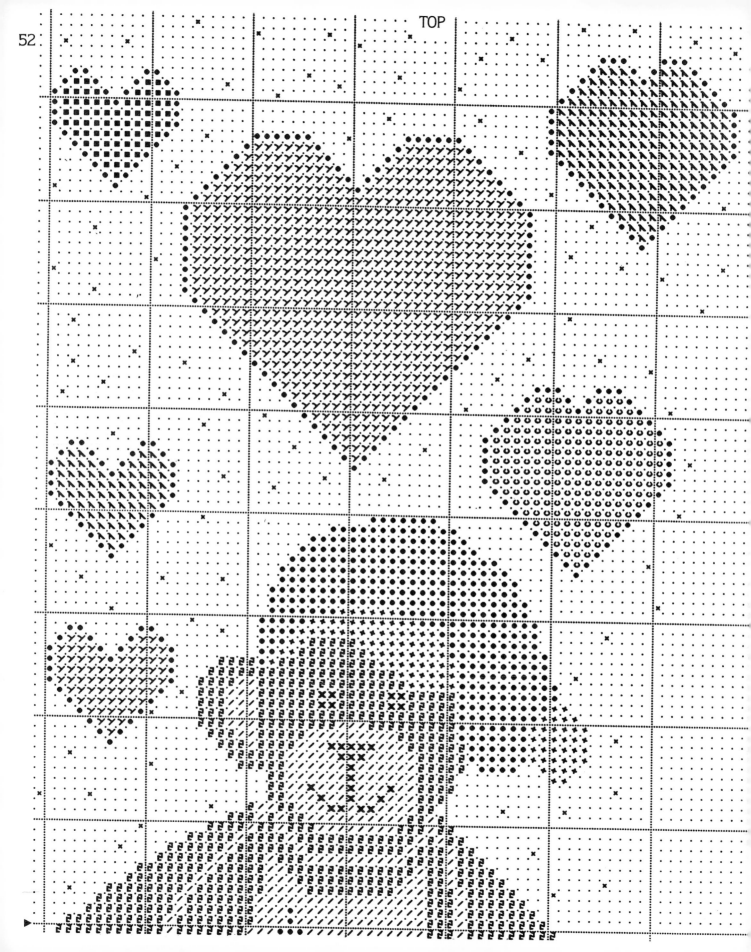

TOP

BOTTOM

DANCING GNOMES WITH BASKETS STOCKING

● *Gnomes always played an important part in my life when I was growing up in Sweden. At Christmastime, gnomes were as special as Santa himself.*

Here they are on the mantel—merry and full of mischief. We've let them loose on this stocking to dance with a basket, candle, gift package and balls.

It's not necessary to fill in the entire background. You can follow the chart exactly—cross-stitch one row around each gnome and star. A blue fabric can also be used, if you feel that there is too much background to stitch.

**DANCING GNOMES
WITH BASKETS STOCKING**

Cut size: 20″ × 14″
Finished size: 14″ long;
              8″ wide at top.

#18 even-weave linen
  4 strands of floss

	DMC#	
●●●●●●	349	red
◆◆◆◆◆◆	948	flesh
ʏʏʏʏʏʏ	973	med. yellow
×××××	725	gold
ʏʏʏʏʏʏ	782	bronze
▽▽▽▽▽▽	783	gold ochre
×××××	823	deep ultramarine blue
ʌʌʌʌʌʌ	701	green
■■■■■■	824	dk. blue
✦✦✦✦✦✦		white
‿‿‿‿‿	823	deep ultramarine blue backstitch

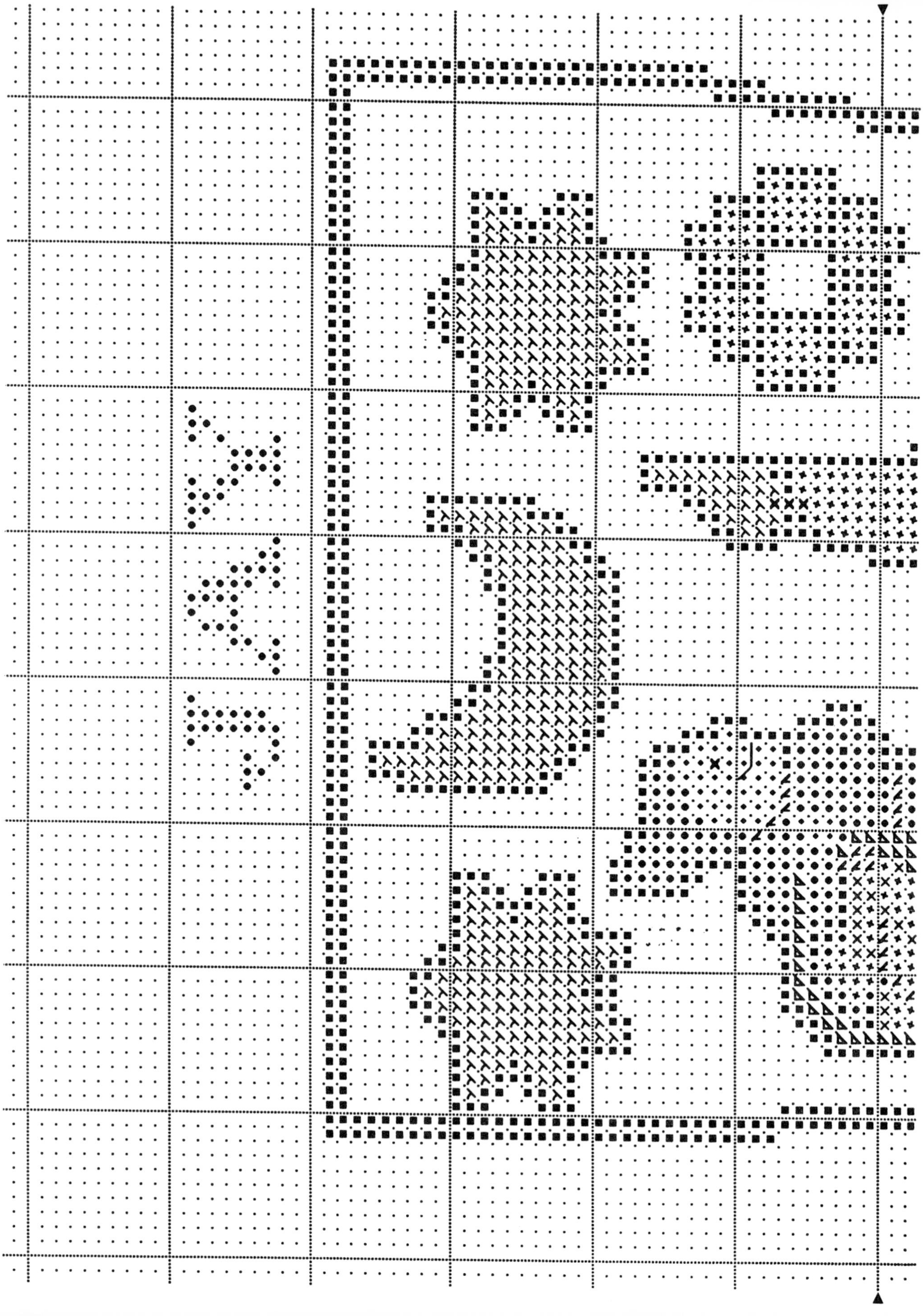

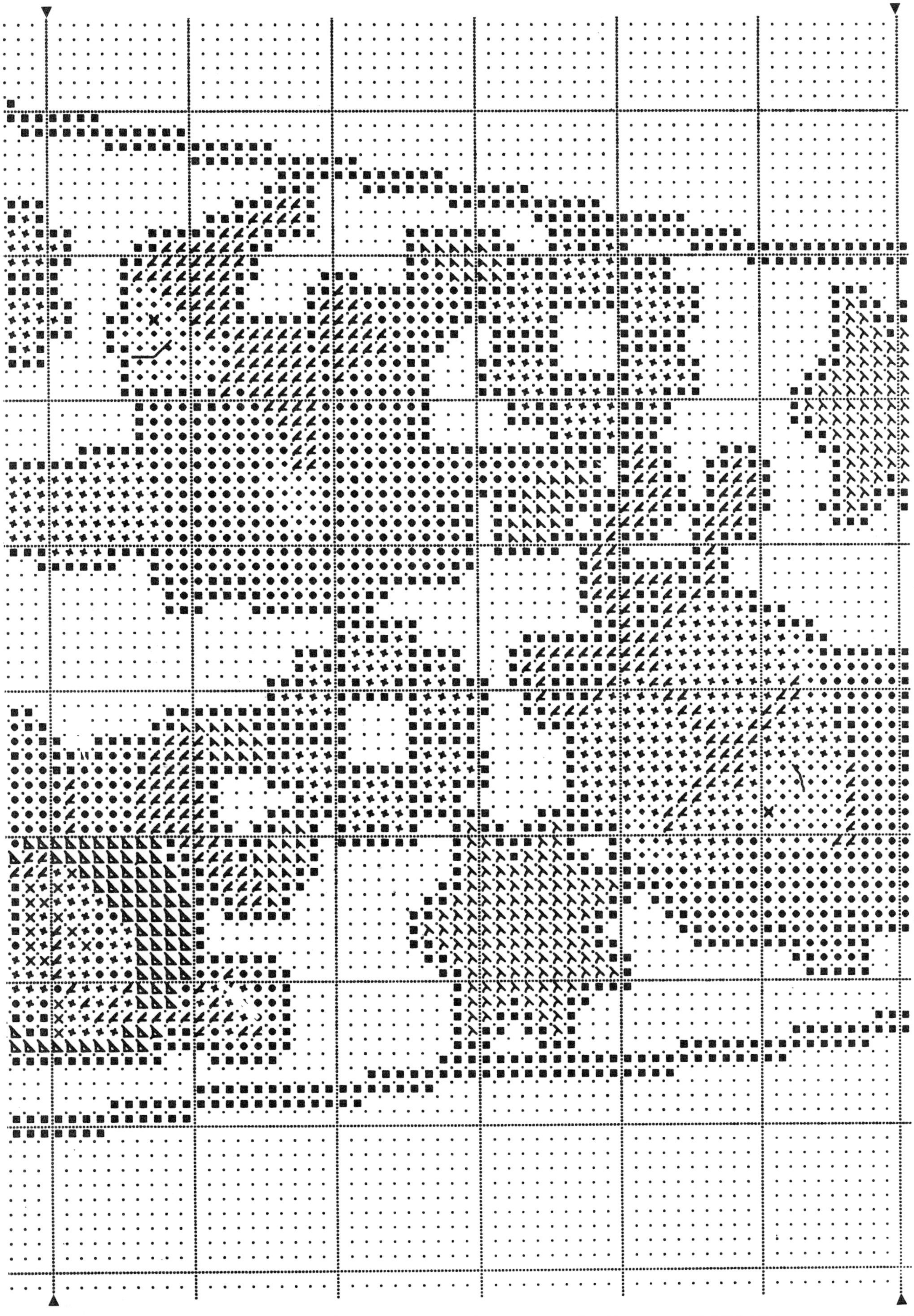

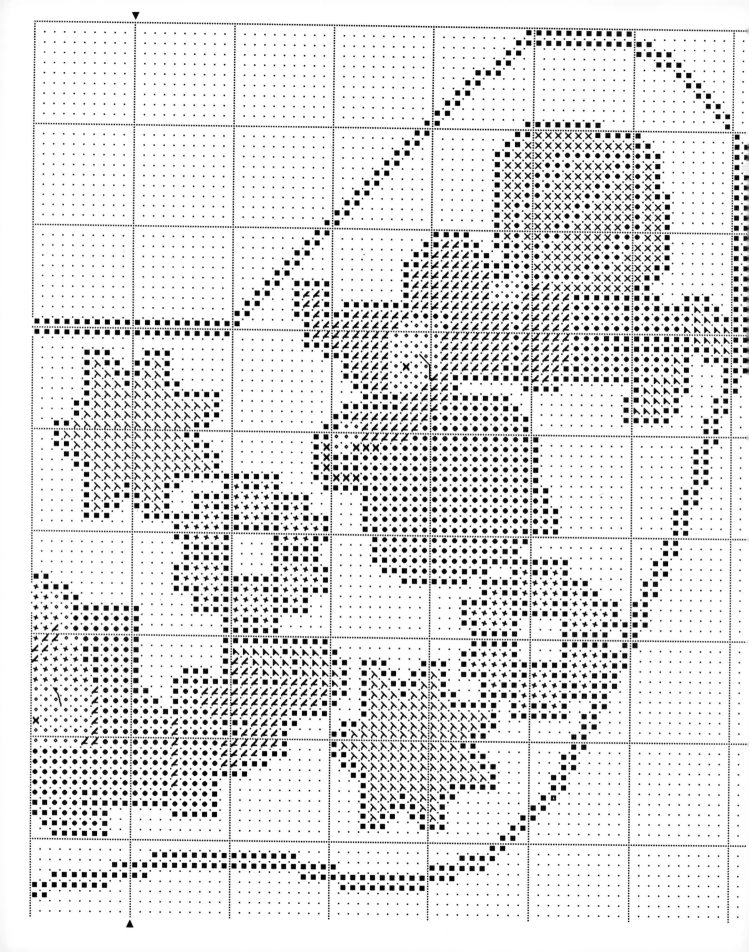

COUNTRY CHRISTMAS TABLES

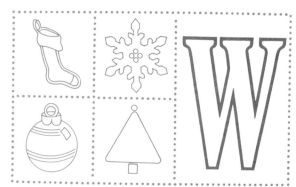

WHEATSTALKS AND BOWS TABLECLOTH

● There is something very special about an embroidered Christmas tablecloth. Sweet smelling pies, richly flavored eggnog in cut glass punch bowls, and a thick, moist Christmas pudding all seem more festive and wonderful when they're set on this cloth. A truly splendid heirloom that can be passed from generation to generation.

The tablecloth has been designed so that it is suitable for a round, square or rectangular table.

Take your time on this project. It is a treasure well worth all your effort.

WHEATSTALKS AND BOWS TABLECLOTH
Cut size: 76″ × 54″
Finished size: 72″ × 50″

#18 even-weave linen
 4 strands of floss

	DMC#	
●●●●●	349	red
×××××	725	gold
▫▫▫▫▫	912	emerald
———	823	deep ultramarine blue backstitch

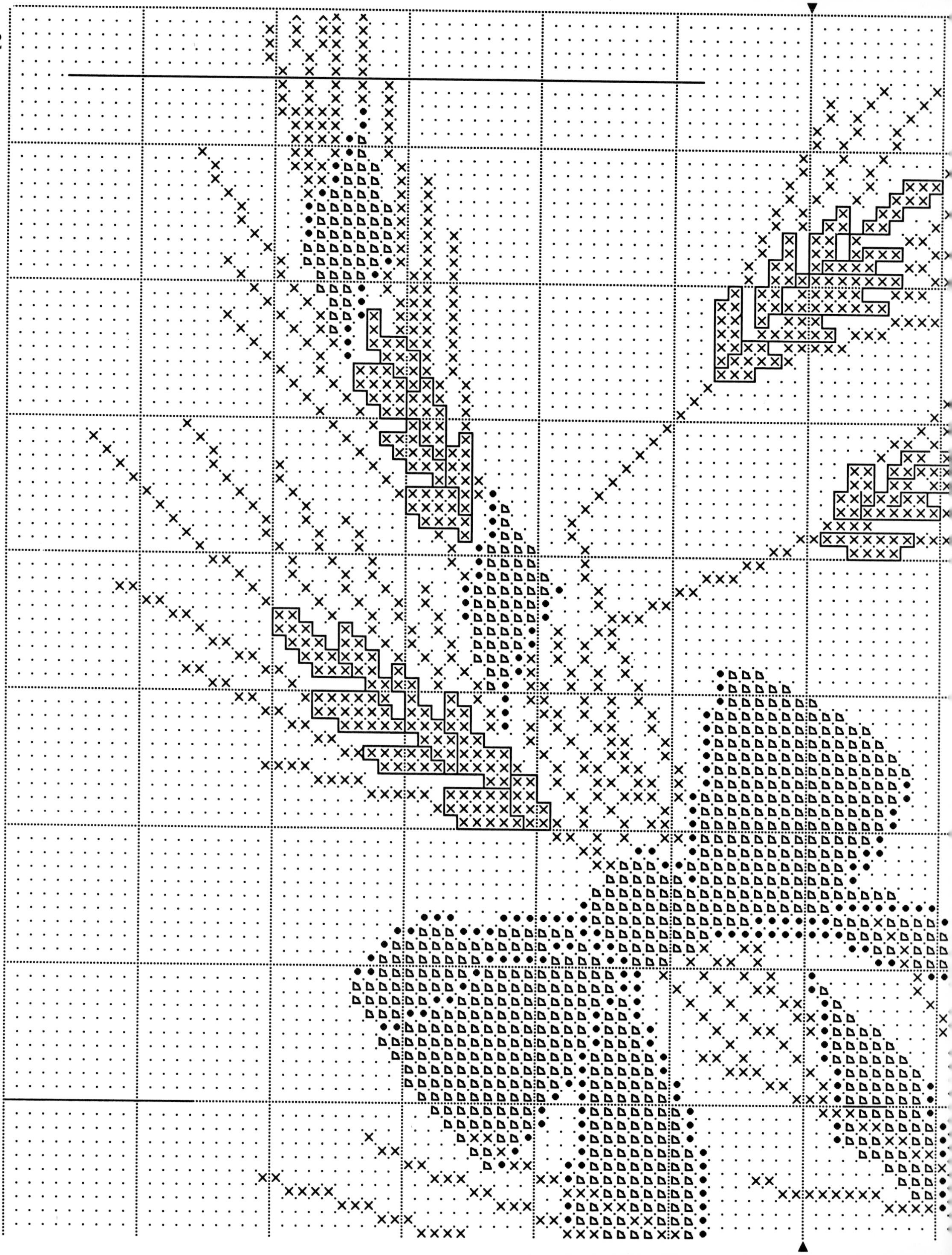

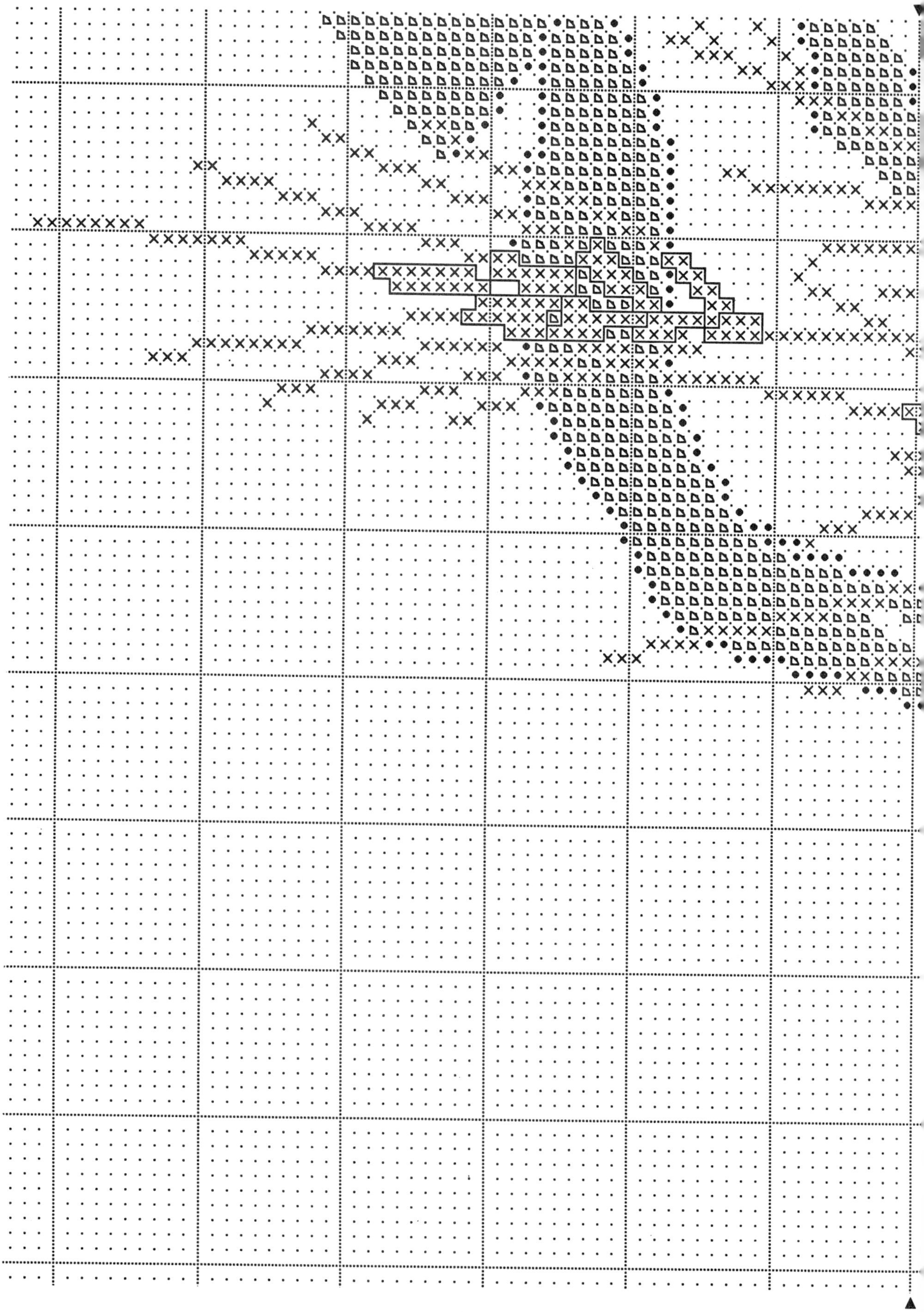

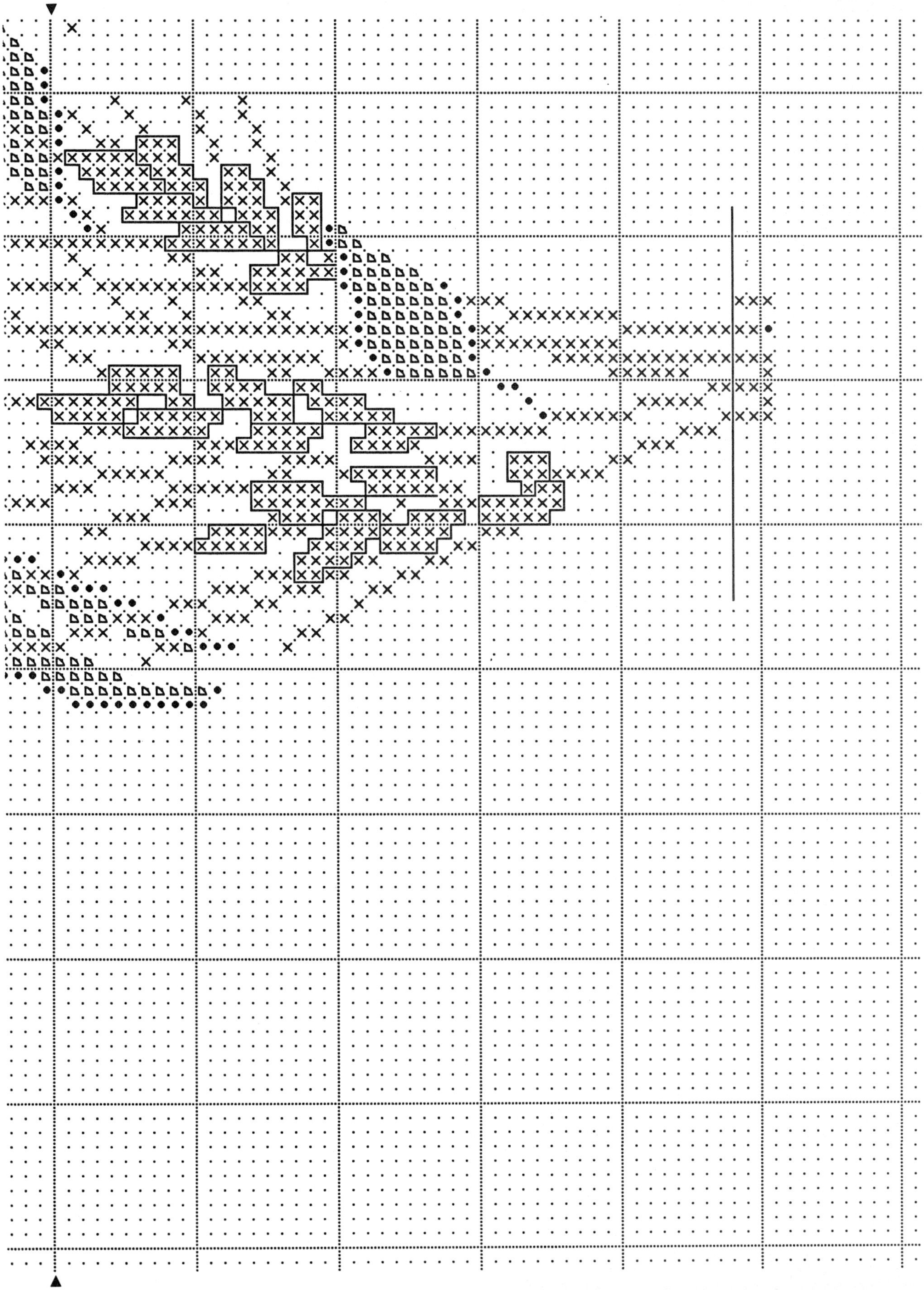

HEARTS AND WREATHS TABLECLOTH

● *This tablecloth has a light, contemporary feeling, and the design is mirror imaged. If you want to simplify the design, you can do so by cross-stitching two images—the right and left.*

The pattern is suitable for a square or rectangular table.

HEARTS AND WREATHS TABLECLOTH

Cut size: 76″ × 54″
Finished size: 72″ × 50″

#18 even-weave linen
    4 strands of floss

	DMC#	
●●●●●●	349	red
⁊⁊⁊⁊⁊⁊	307	lt. yellow
ꙮꙮꙮꙮꙮꙮ	400	chestnut
◌◌◌◌◌◌	912	emerald

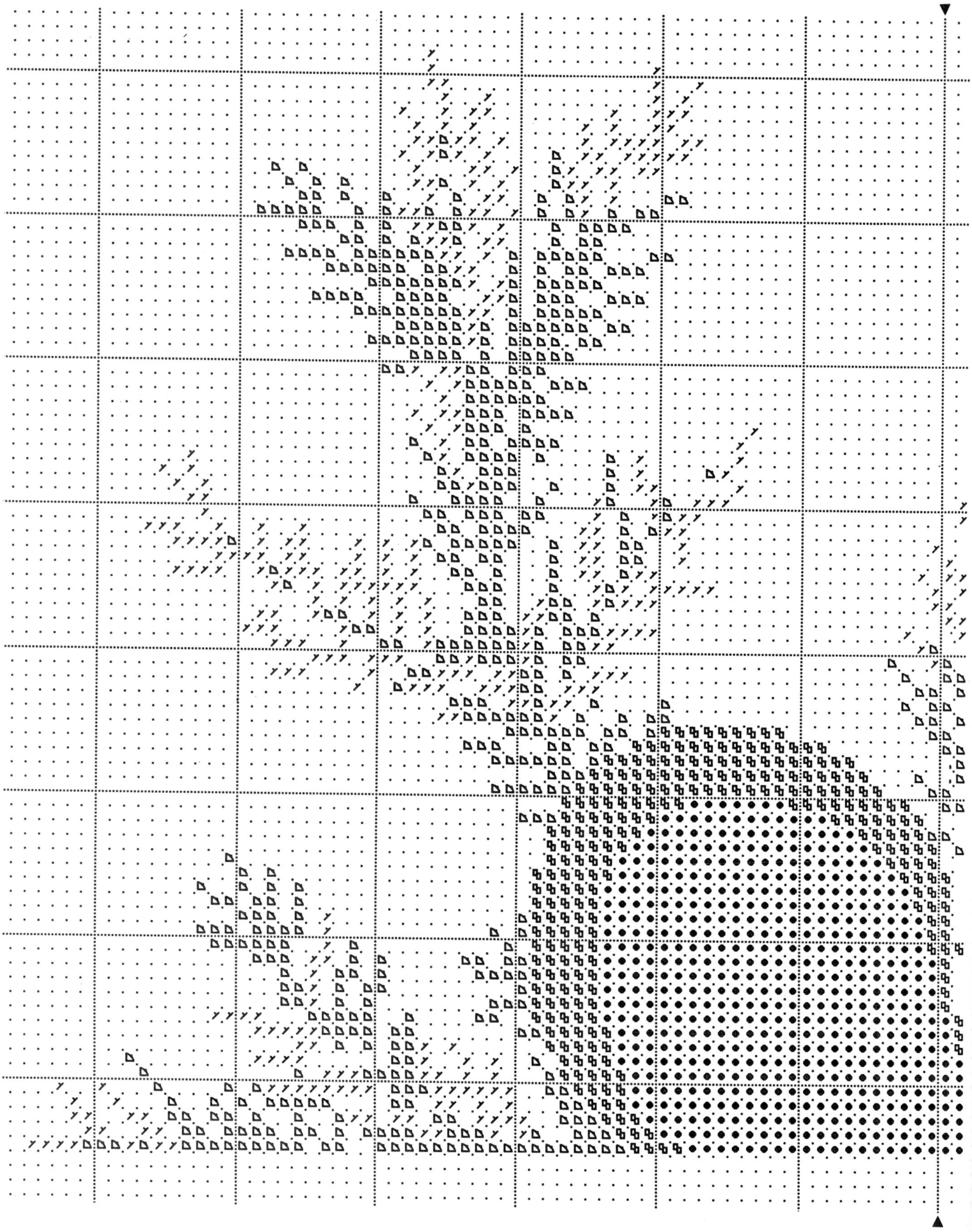

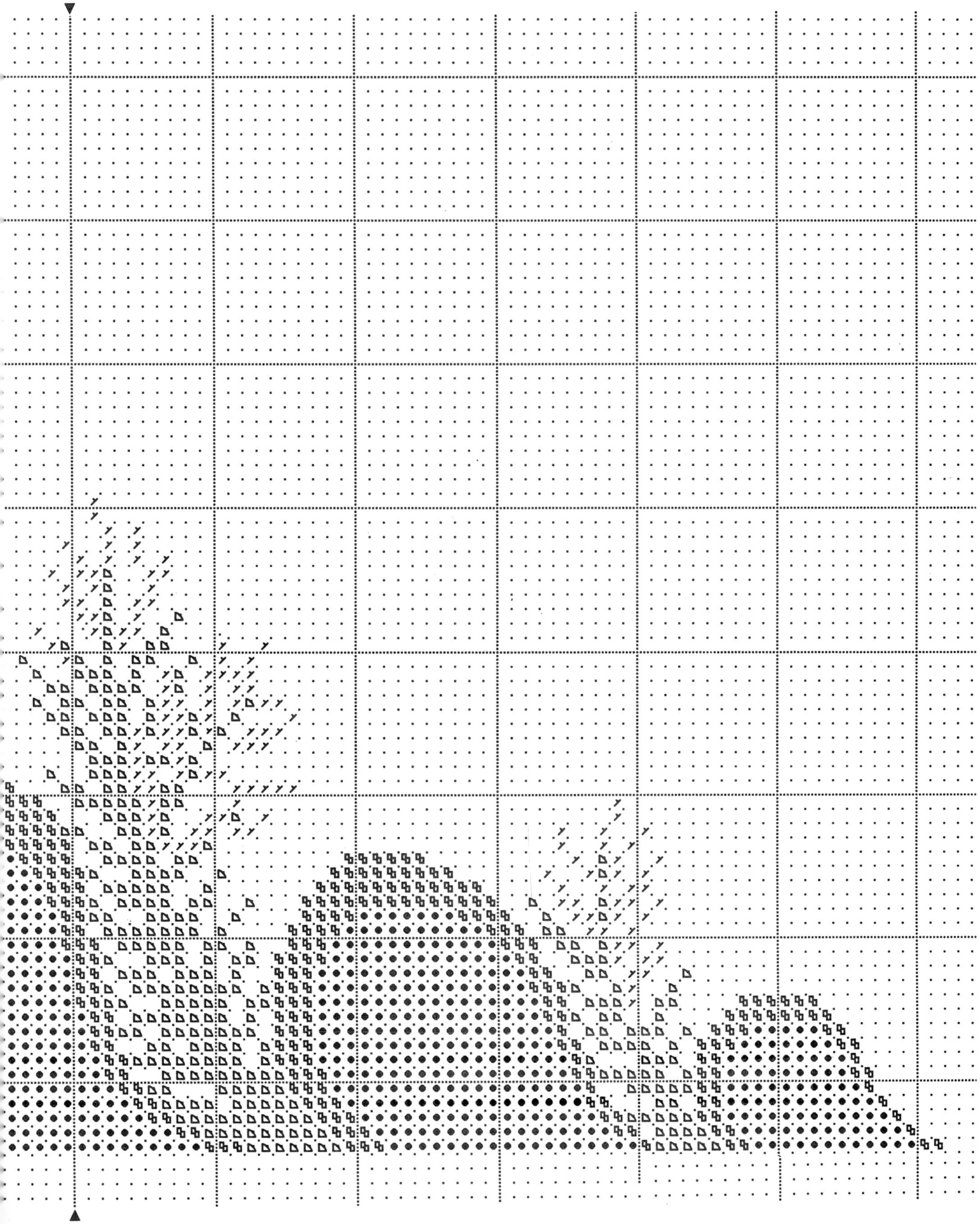

PINE CONE RUNNER

● *An exquisite stretch of pine cones can grace an entryway table, a mantelpiece or a windowsill. Use your imagination. And since the pattern is repeated, you can make it any length you desire.*

PINE CONE RUNNER

Cut size: 14″ × 40″
Finished size: 10″ × 36″

#18 even-weave linen
 4 strands of floss

	DMC#	
๖๖๖๖๖	400	chestnut
ʌʌʌʌʌ	701	med. green
ᵥᵥᵥᵥᵥ	907	chartreuse

72

center

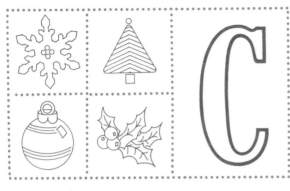

CHRISTMAS BALL ORNAMENTS RUNNER

• Deck the halls with Christmas balls! Ornaments are not just for the tree. Here we've put them on a fanciful runner, that will add a cheery note to any table. Personally, I like this design very much. It's colorful, direct and up-beat.

The design is a repeat pattern, so you can make this runner any length you want.

CHRISTMAS BALL ORNAMENTS RUNNER

Cut size: 14″ × 40″
Finished size: 10″ × 36″

#18 even-weave linen
  4 strands of floss

	DMC#	
● ● ● ● ●	349	red
✗ ✗ ✗ ✗ ✗	321	scarlet
▽ ▽ ▽ ▽ ▽	783	gold ochre
⋀ ⋀ ⋀ ⋀ ⋀	701	med. green

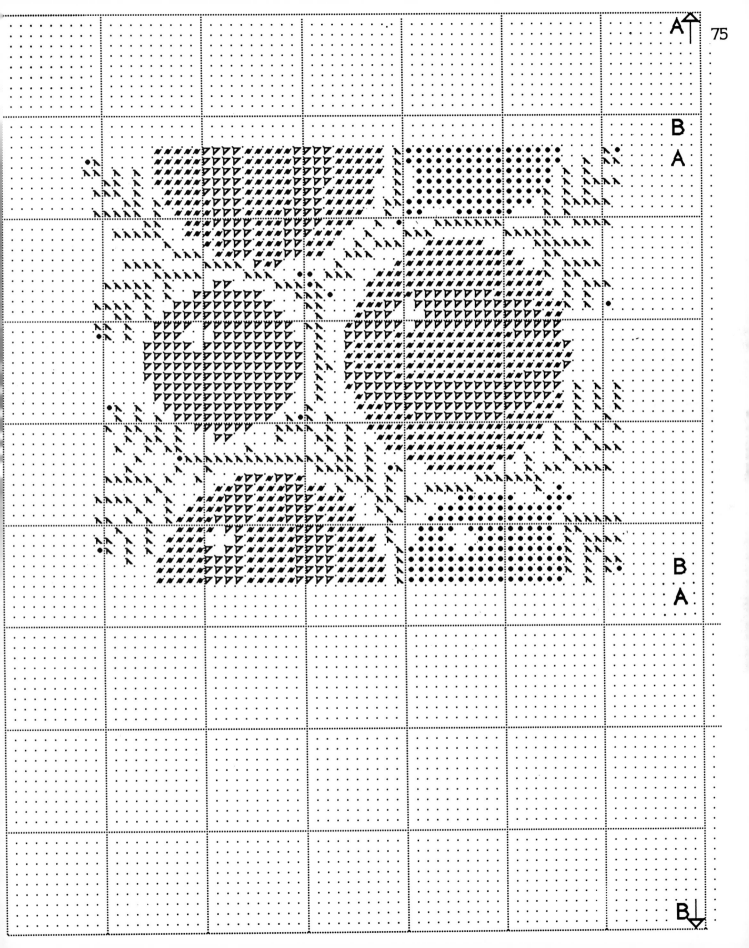

CRANBERRIES AND LEAVES PLACE MATS AND NAPKINS

● *If you don't have time to make a tablecloth this year, there is always time to make a few place mats and napkins. Our cranberries are fast and easy-to-make. A set of two place mats and napkins would make a thoughtful gift.*

In addition to this design, flip through the book for other ideas. A pine cone, candleholder, candy cane or bell would make suitable motifs for Christmas place mats and napkins.

CRANBERRIES AND LEAVES PLACE MATS AND NAPKINS

Cut size: place mat   16″ × 22″
              napkin   16″ × 12″

Finished size: place mat 12″ × 18″
                   napkin   12″ × 8″

#18 even-weave linen
  4 strands of floss

	DMC#	
✓✓✓✓✓	321	scarlet
✗✗✗✗✗	989	med. olive
ʟʟʟʟʟ	907	chartreuse

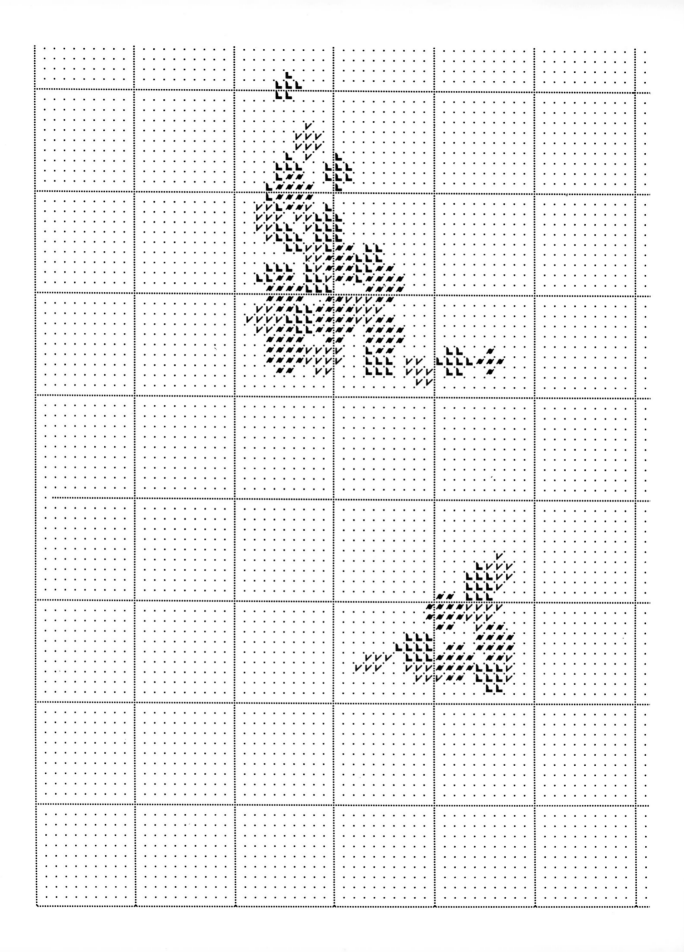

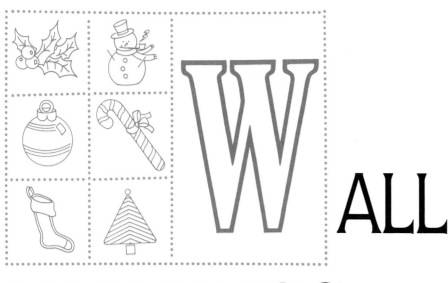

WALL HANGINGS

HEARTS ADVENT CALENDAR

● *For children of all ages. A gift-wrapped present or a piece of candy every day for the twenty-four days before Christmas—each hung from a tiny ring. This advent calendar is a truly wonderful way to share the anticipation and joy of giving with children, while they eagerly await Christmas day.*

When I was growing up, we were given a proverb or saying for each day. These meaningful words were written in wildly curling script on parchment paper, and rolled and tied with a red satin ribbon. Through the years, these mottos have become a part of my life. Many are well-remembered, and they are the ones that I live by.

HEARTS ADVENT CALENDA

Cut size: 20″ × 12″
Finished size: 15″ × 8″

#18 even-weave linen
4 strands of floss

	DMC#	
● ● ● ● ●	349	red
♠ ♠ ♠ ♠ ♠	598	aquamarine
▫ ▫ ▫ ▫ ▫	799	med. blue

82

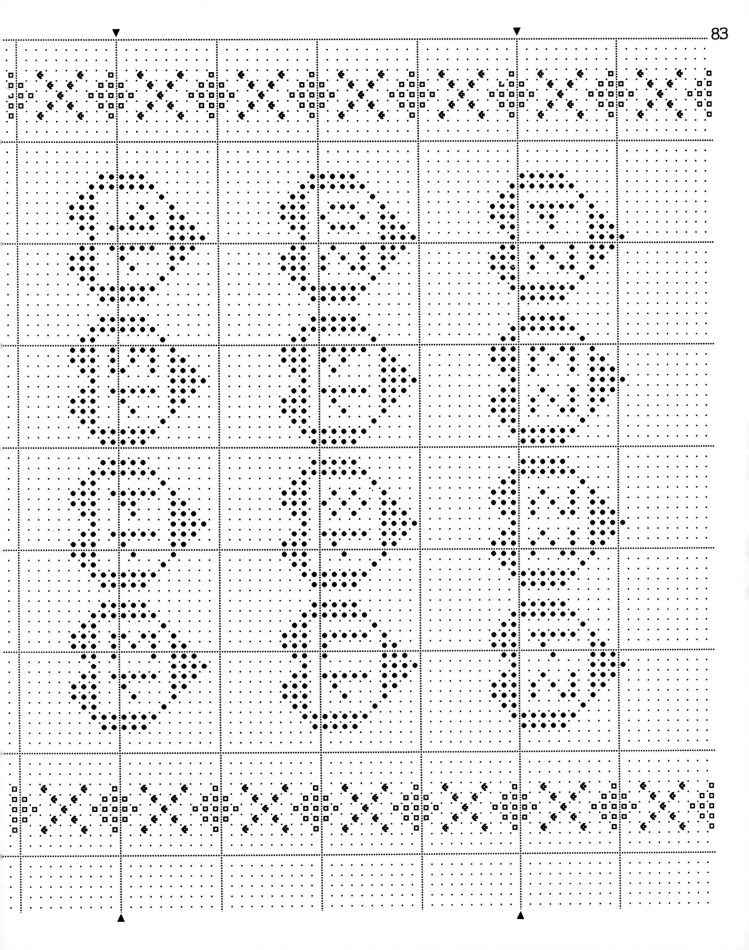

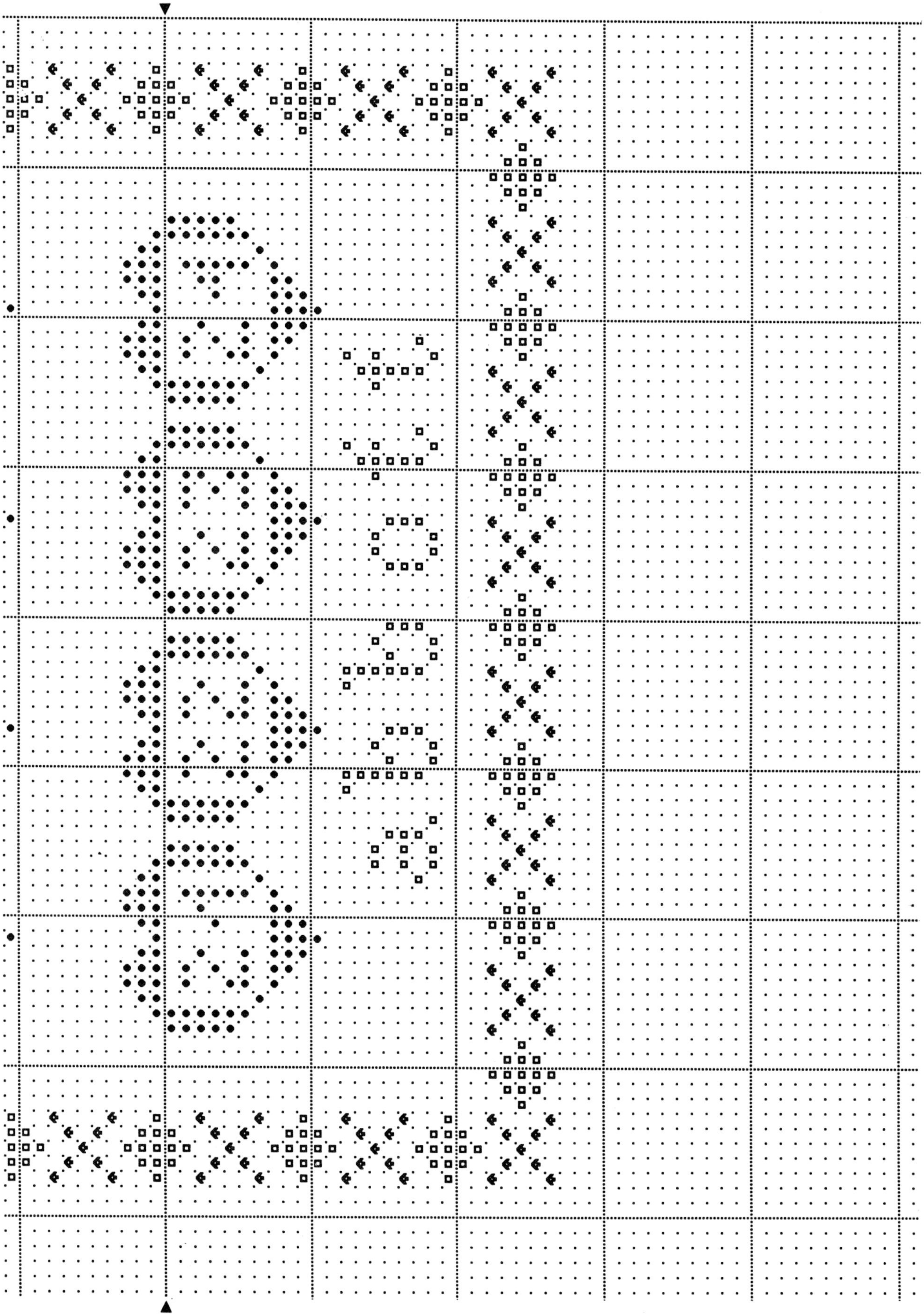

GINGERBREAD HOUSE

• *Who can resist the charm of a gingerbread house? The advantage of a cross-stitched gingerbread house is that it is easy to store, and it can be brought out Christmas after Christmas to decorate your home. You may not be able to munch on this house, but the "cinnamon-y" richness and warmth will be apparent, no matter where you place this wall hanging.*

GINGERBREAD HOUSE

Cut size: 16″ × 14″
Finished size: 12″ × 9″

#18 even-weave linen
4 strands of floss
3 yd. gold metallic thread

	DMC#	
●●●●●	349	red
○○○○○	819	pink
YYYYY	973	med. yellow
▚▚▚▚▚	400	chestnut
⋏⋏⋏⋏⋏	701	med. green
▪▪▪▪▪	827	lt. blue
♦♦♦♦♦	208	lilac
+++++		white
÷÷÷÷÷		gold metallic

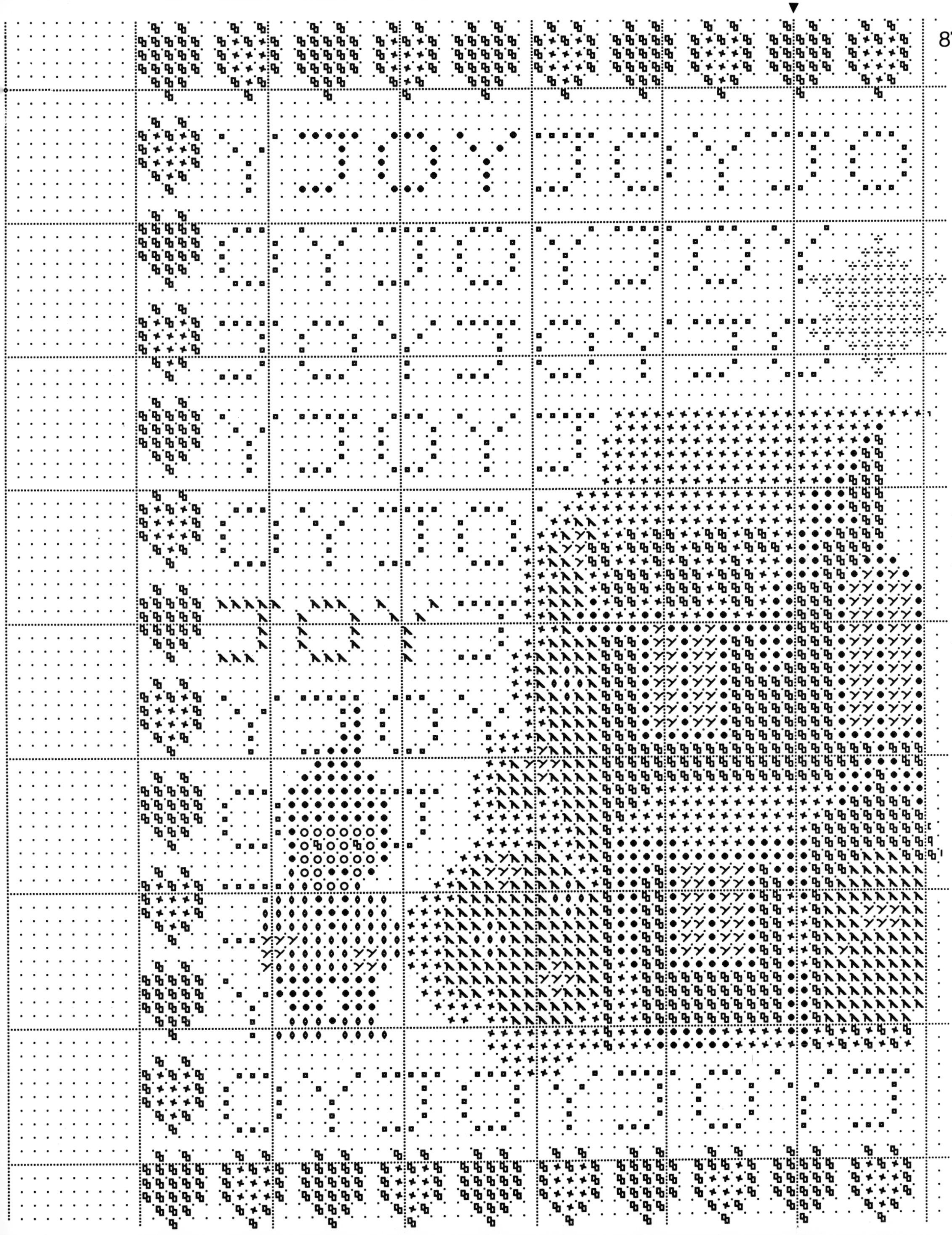

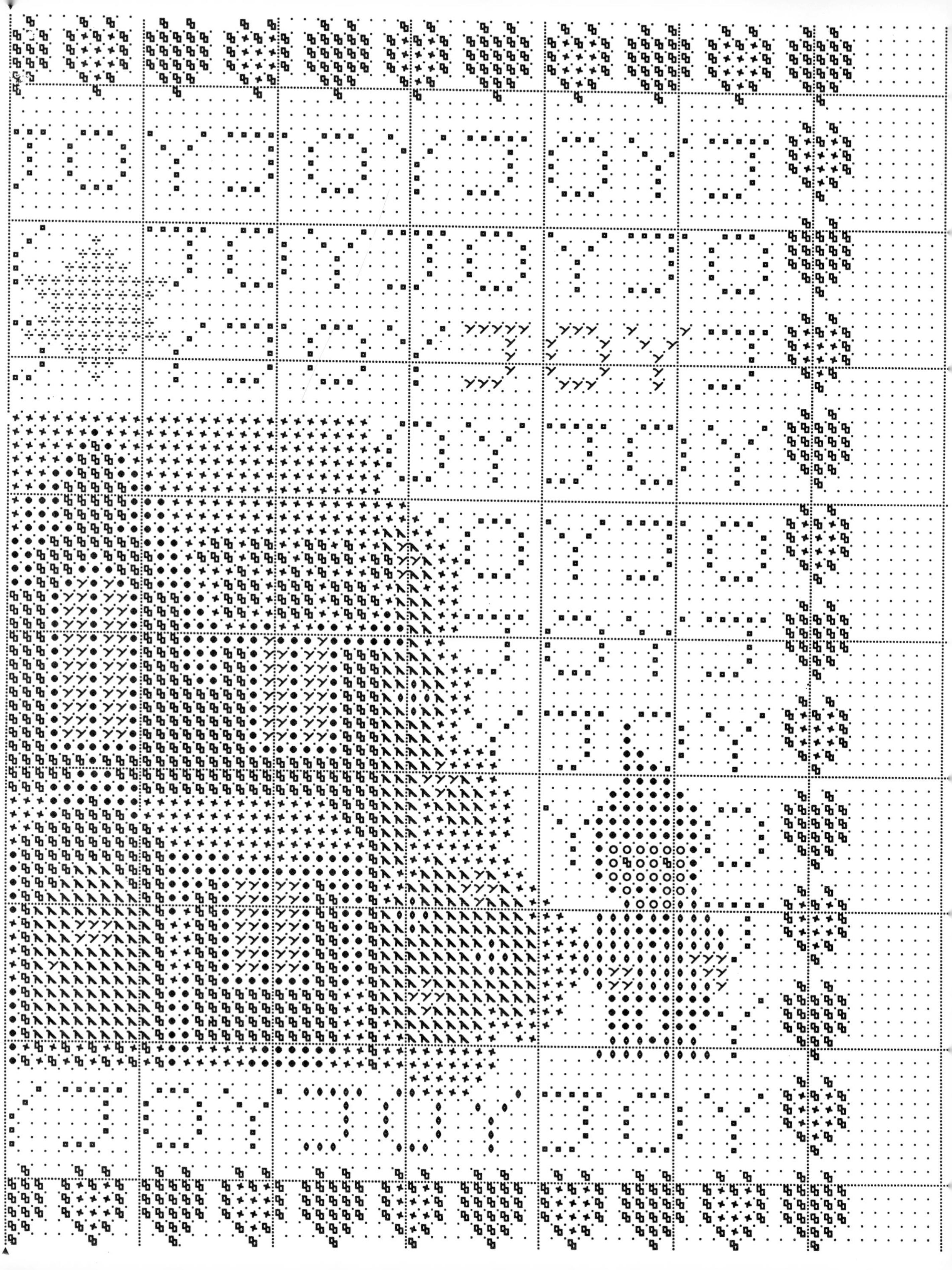

WELCOME

SAMPLER

● *We chose a very Victorian lettering for this sampler. Hang it in your entryway or over a buffet table. It is a genuine invitation to share all the pleasures of the season. Make this very special hanging to greet your family and friends, and to welcome the spirit of Christmas into your home.*

WELCOME SAMPLER

Cut size: 17″ × 13″
Finished size: 13″ × 9″

#18 even-weave linen
4 strands of floss

DMC#
●●●●●● 349 red
ʌʌʌʌʌʌ 701 med. green

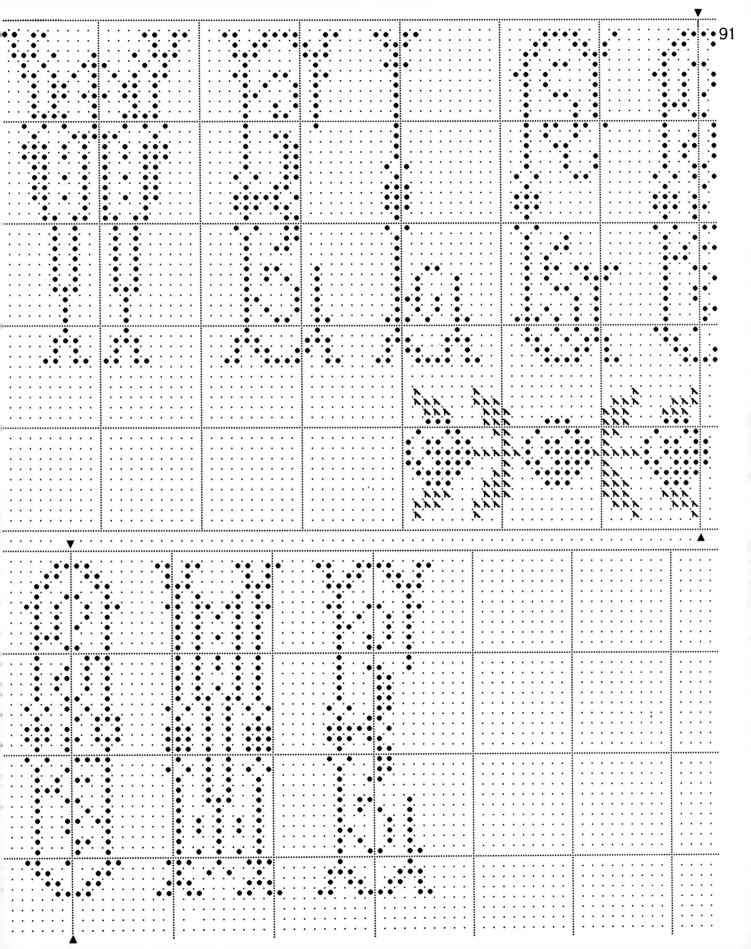

BABY'S FIRST CHRISTMAS—TEDDY BEAR AND MOON

● *Nothing could be a more perfect "first Christmas" present. Personalize and date it (See Alphabet and Numbers, page 187) for the new baby in your life. Definitely an heirloom that will become more meaningful and treasured for years to come.*

**BABY'S FIRST CHRISTMAS—
TEDDY BEAR AND MOON**

Cut size: 16″ × 16″
Finished size: 12″ × 12″

#18 even-weave linen
  4 strands of floss
  4 yd. silver metallic thread

	DMC#	
ʌʌʌʌʌʌ	701	med. green
xxxxxx	823	deep ultramarine blue
●●●●●●	349	red
♠♠♠♠♠♠	598	aquamarine
■■■■■■	824	dk. blue
▽▽▽▽▽▽	783	gold ochre
oooooo	819	pink
x x x x x		silver metallic

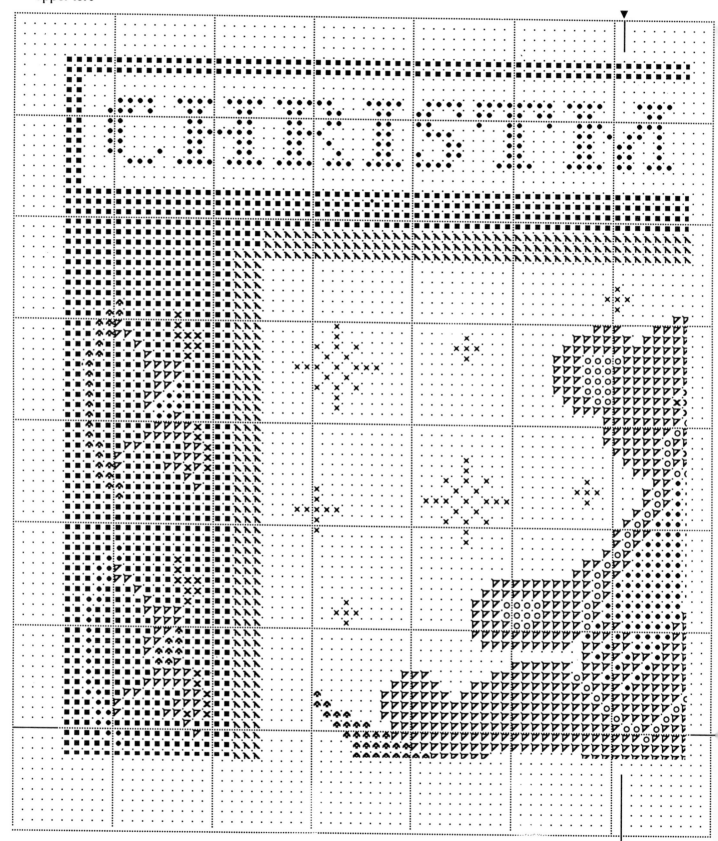

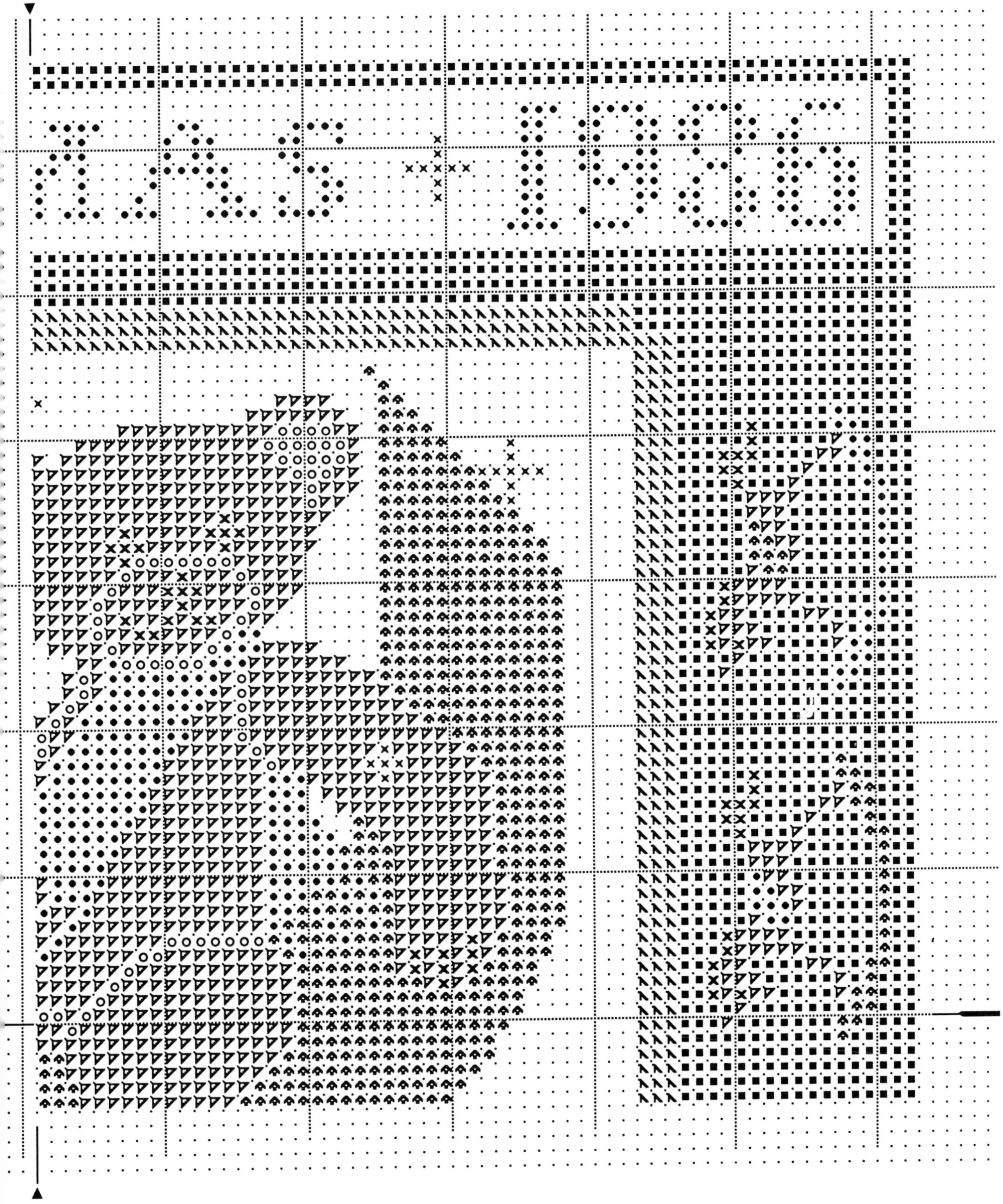

96

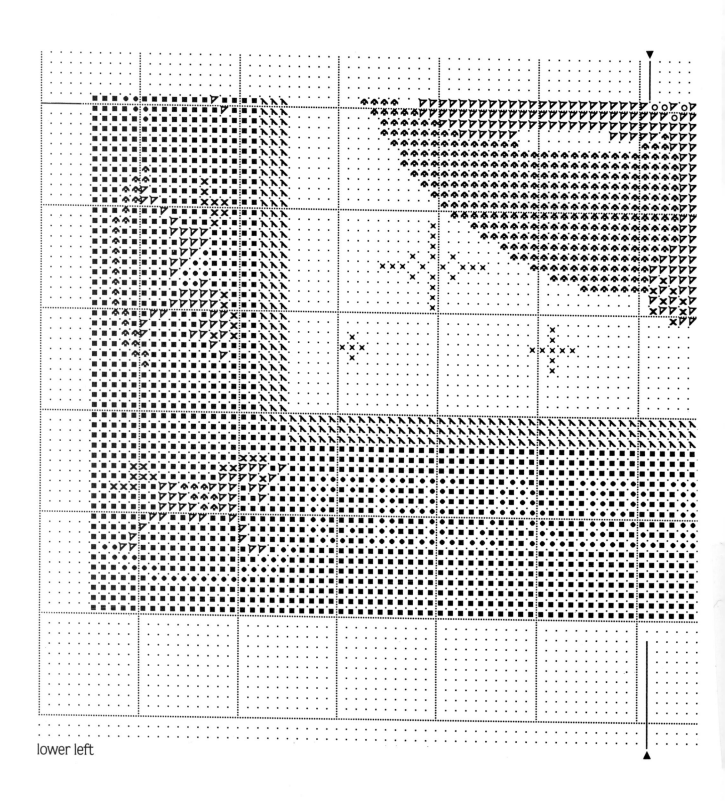

lower left

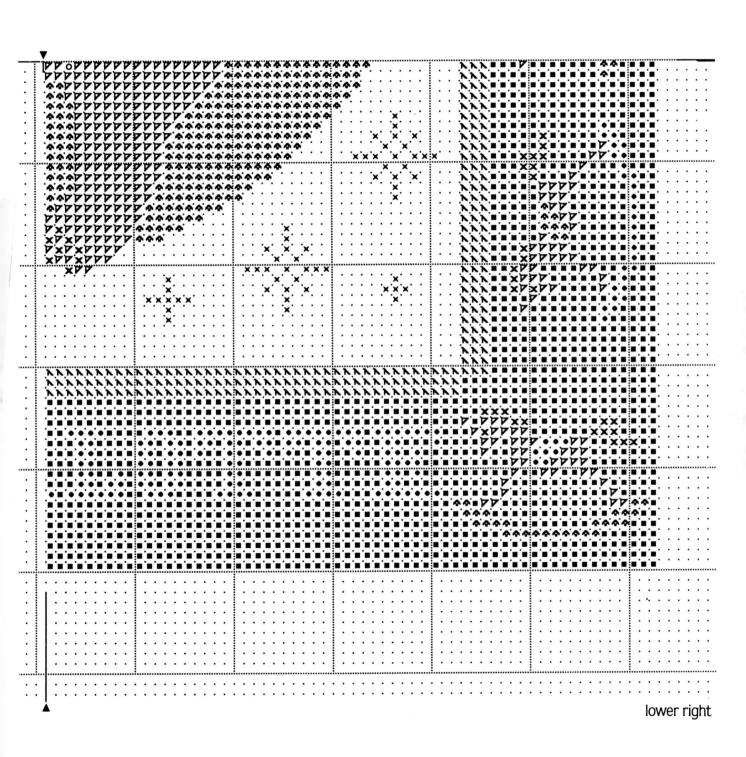

lower right

CHRISTMAS KITTENS

● *A boxful of kittens—a "purr-fect" picture for cat lovers. There's even a tag on the box that can be either personalized or dated.*

These three Christmas kittens will bring you great joy—while you're working on the project, and every time you look at their happy, little faces on the completed wall hanging in your dining or living room.

CHRISTMAS KITTENS

Cut size: 16″ × 17″
Finished size: 12″ × 13″

#18 even-weave linen
4 strands of floss

DMC#

⋏⋏⋏⋏⋏⋏	701	med. green
⋏⋏⋏⋏⋏⋏	3346	dk. olive
૧૧૧૧૧૧	415	dove grey
⋎⋎⋎⋎⋎⋎	973	med. yellow
xxxxx	823	deep ultramarine blue
••••••	349	red
✓✓✓✓✓✓	321	scarlet
▫▫▫▫▫▫	550	dk. purple
⋎⋎⋎⋎⋎⋎	782	bronze
✗✗✗✗✗✗	433	chocolate
▫▫▫▫▫▫	799	med. blue
♠♠♠♠♠♠	598	aquamarine
✦✦✦✦✦✦		white
○○○○○○	819	pink
- - - - - -	799	med. blue backstitch
·-·-·-·-·-	318	med. grey backstitch
────────	823	deep ultramarine blue backstitch

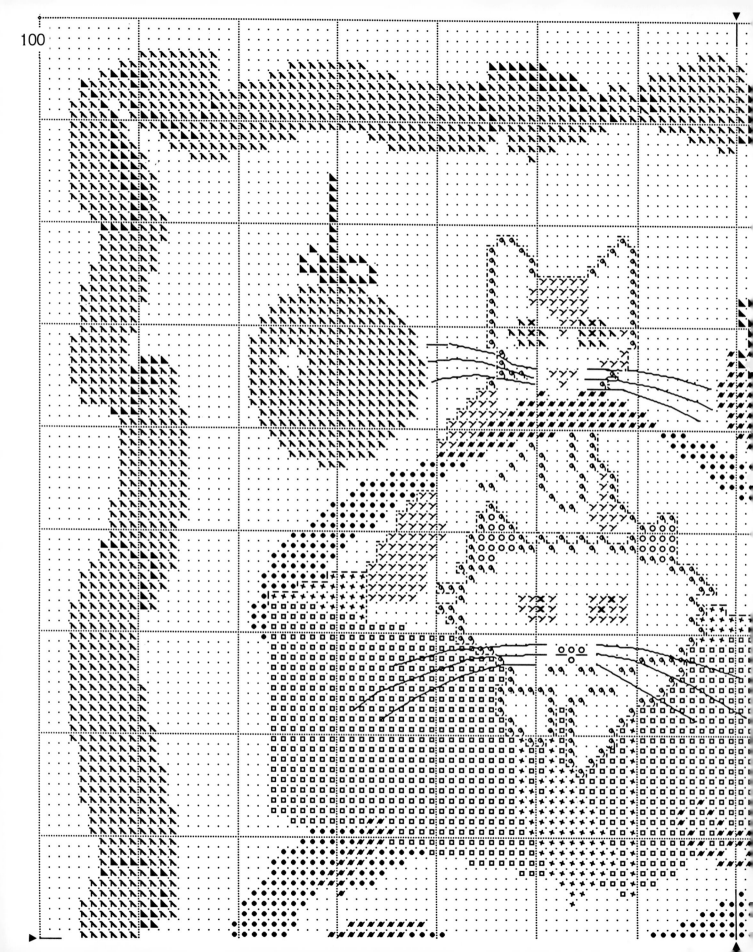

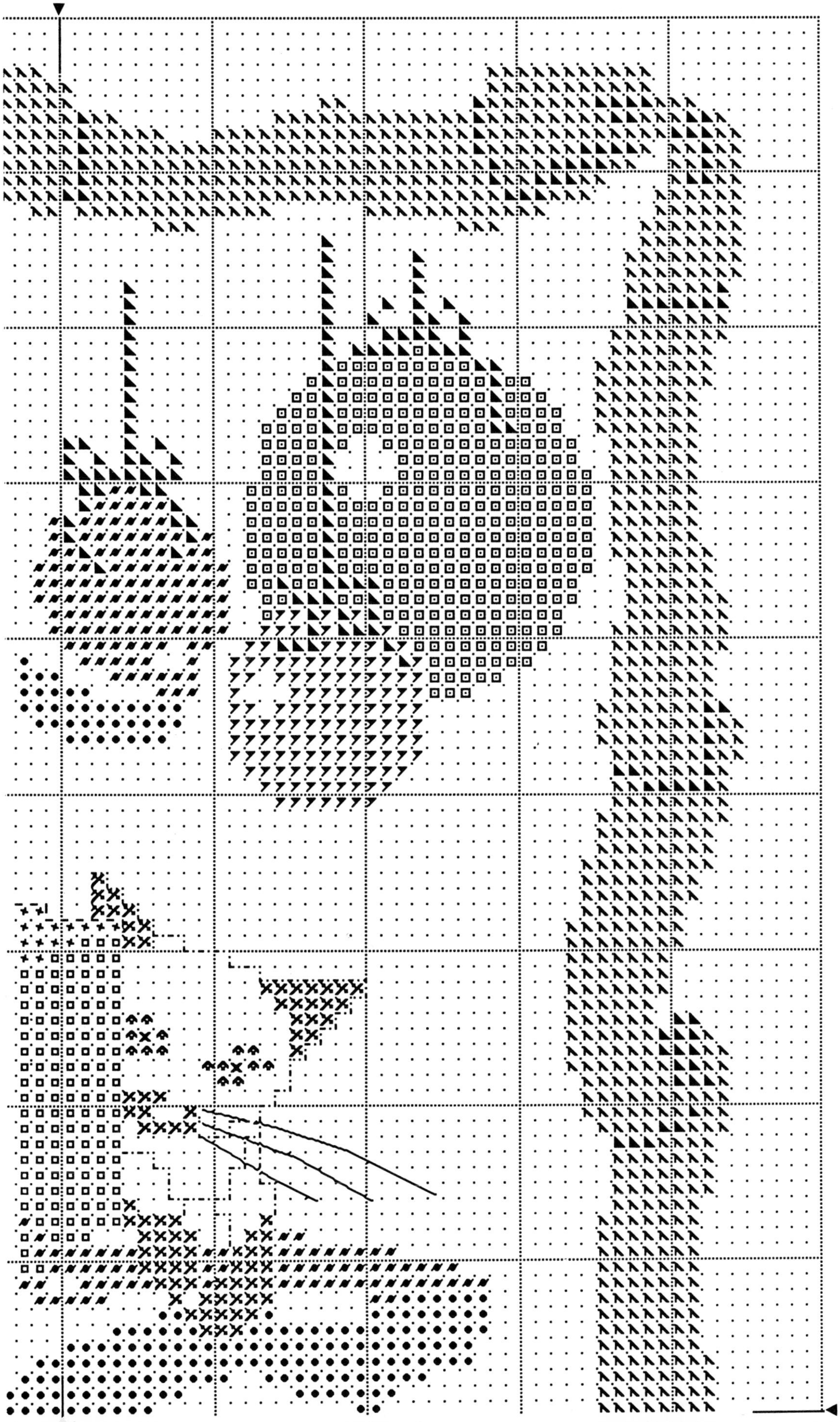

lower
right

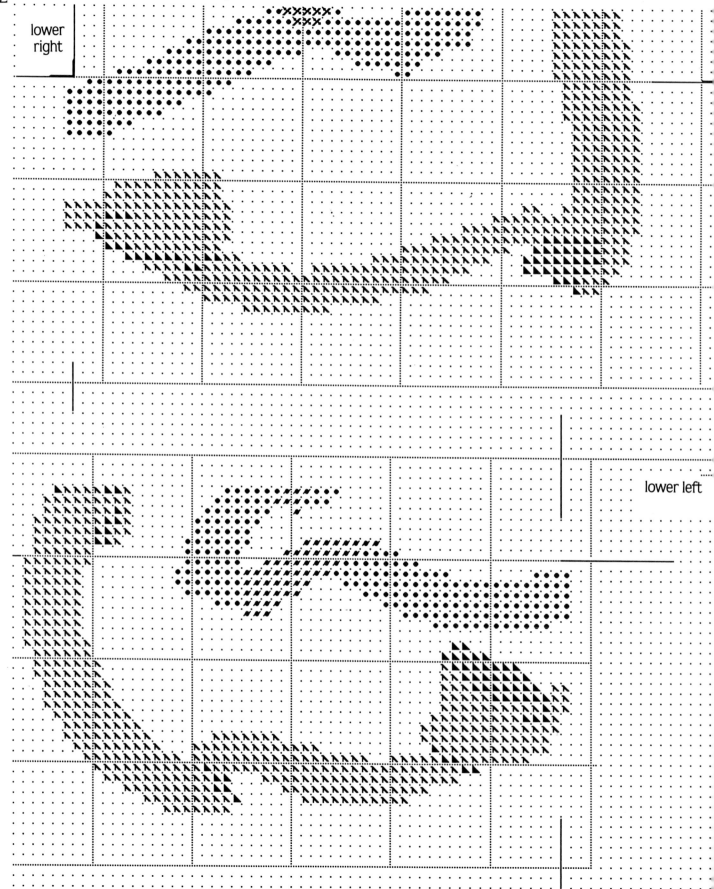

lower left

FRAMED PICTURES

BABY'S FIRST CHRISTMAS—HEARTS

● *Trains, hearts, snowmen, rocking horses and a Christmas angel. You'll love making this simple, contemporary design. And it goes well with any decor. Personalize it, if you like.*

You can substitute the angel design with a name. Or, you can put an angel on either side of the name.

BABY'S FIRST CHRISTMAS— HEARTS

Cut size: 18″ × 24″
Finished size: 14″ × 20″

#18 even-weave linen
  4 strands of floss

	DMC#	
● ● ● ● ●	349	red
◡ ◡ ◡ ◡ ◡	818	med. pink
˅ ˅ ˅ ˅ ˅	973	med. yellow
◇ ◇ ◇ ◇ ◇	922	copper
✕ ✕ ✕ ✕ ✕	433	chocolate
⋀ ⋀ ⋀ ⋀ ⋀	701	med. green
■ ■ ■ ■ ■	824	dk. blue
✕ ✕ ✕ ✕	823	deep ultramarine blue
✦ ✦ ✦ ✦		white
··········	824	dk. blue backstitch
———	823	deep ultramarine blue backstitch

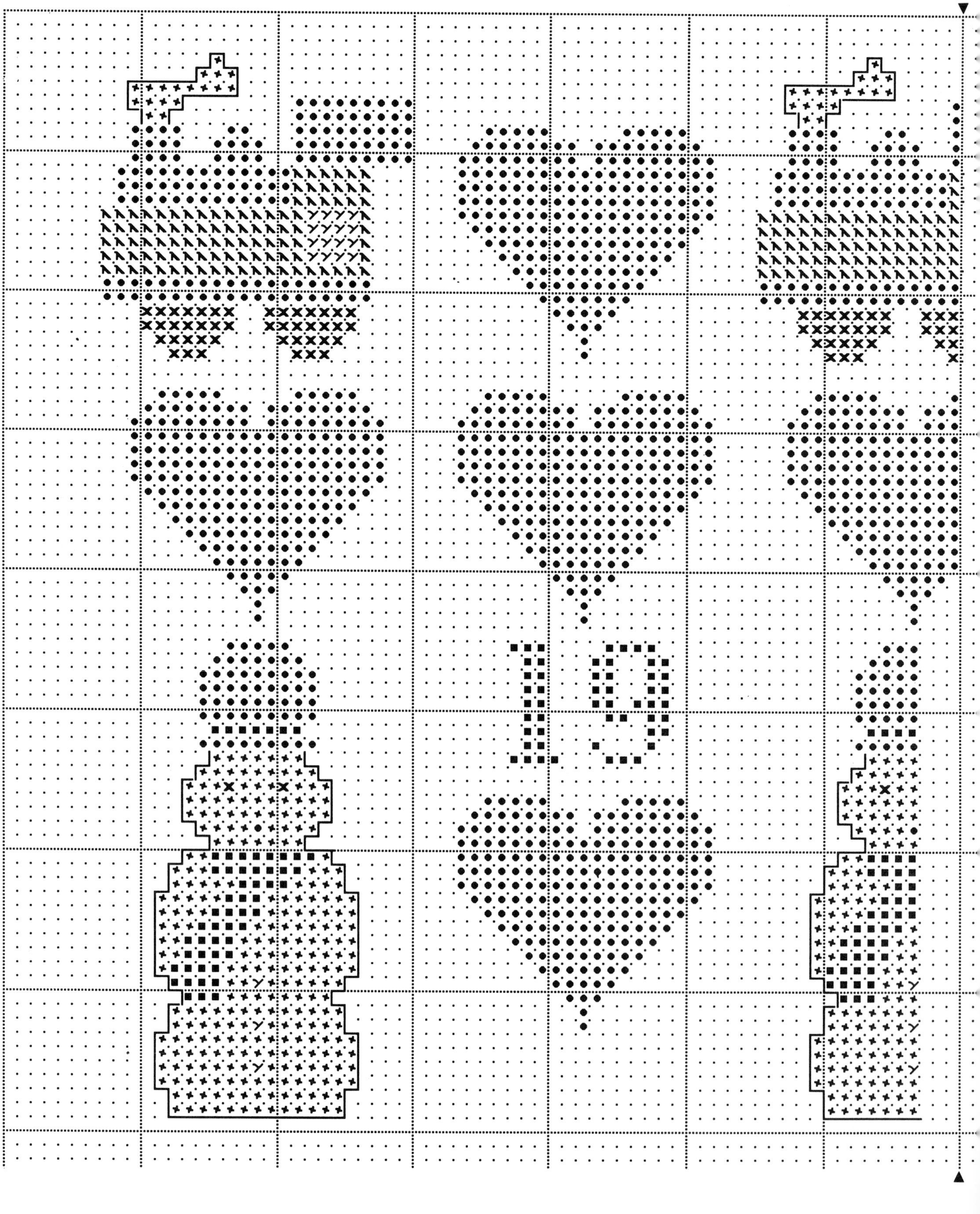

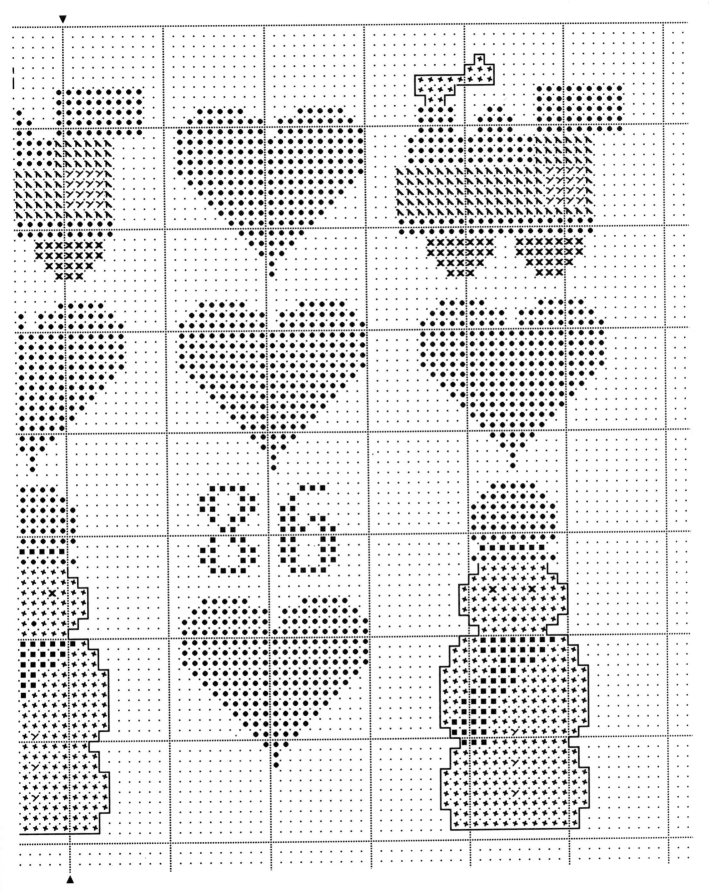

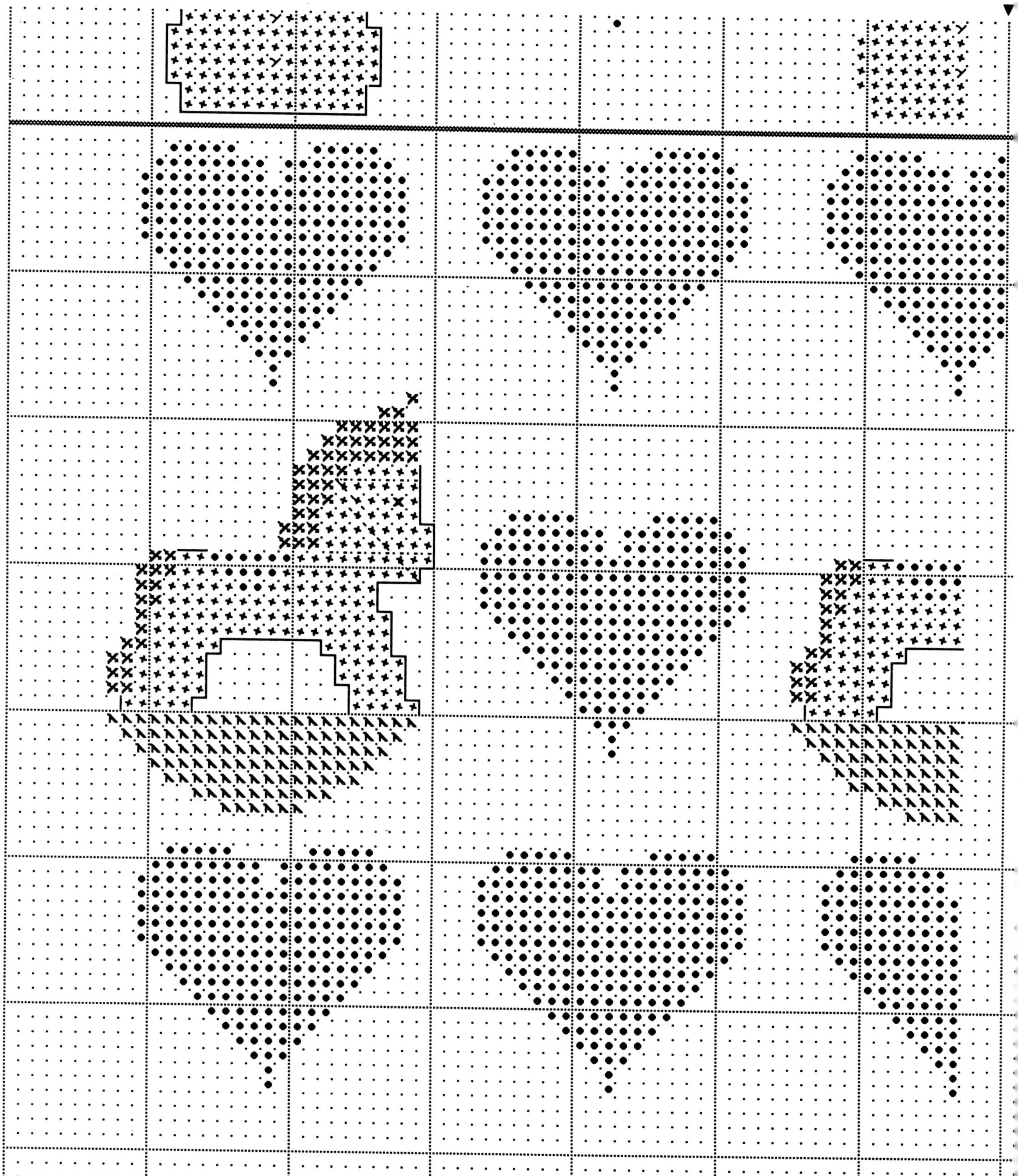

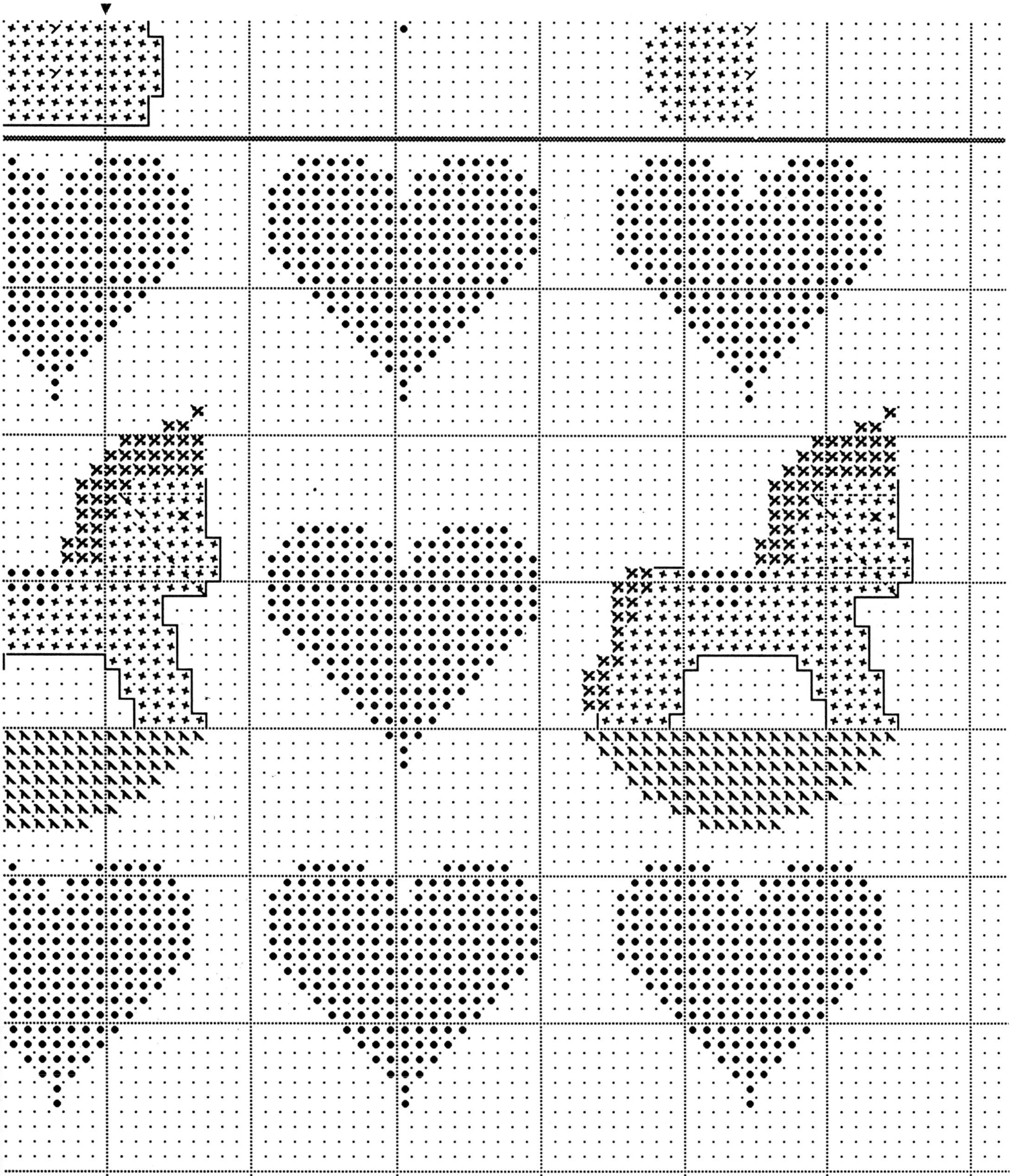

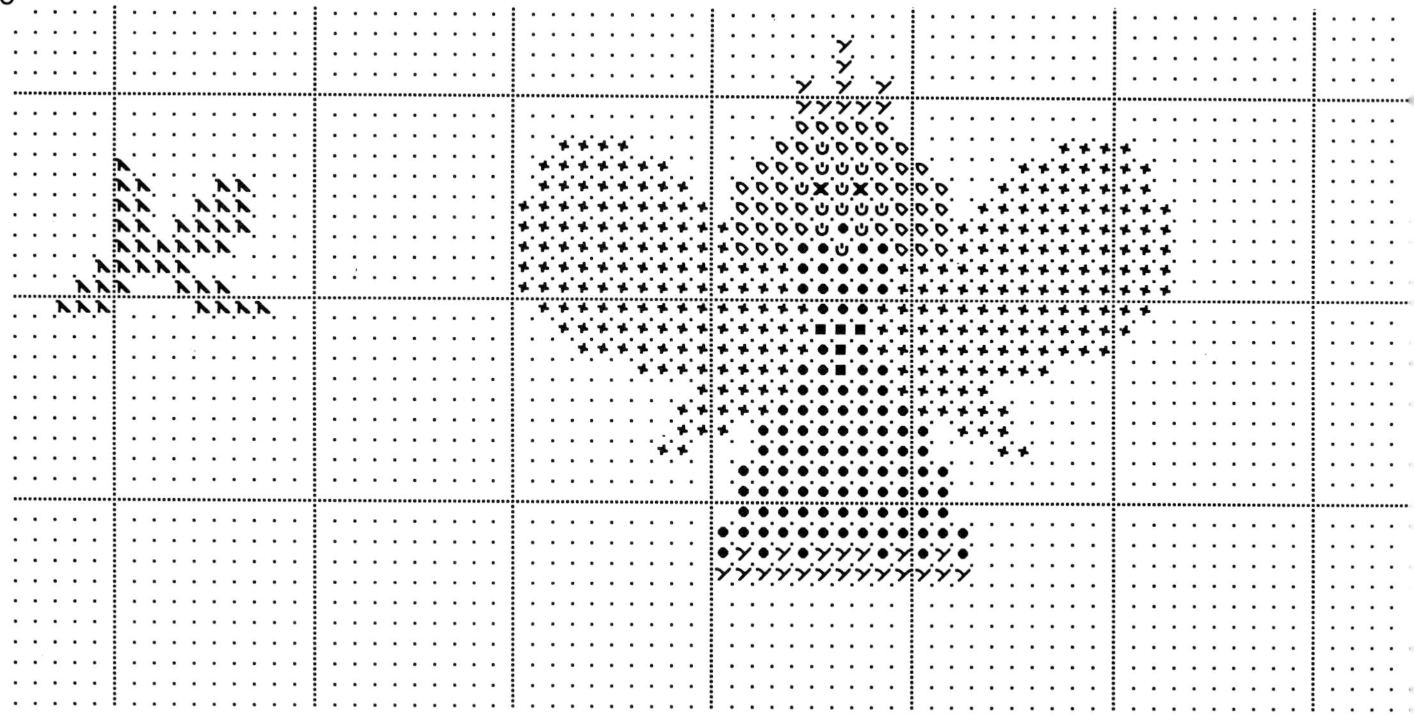

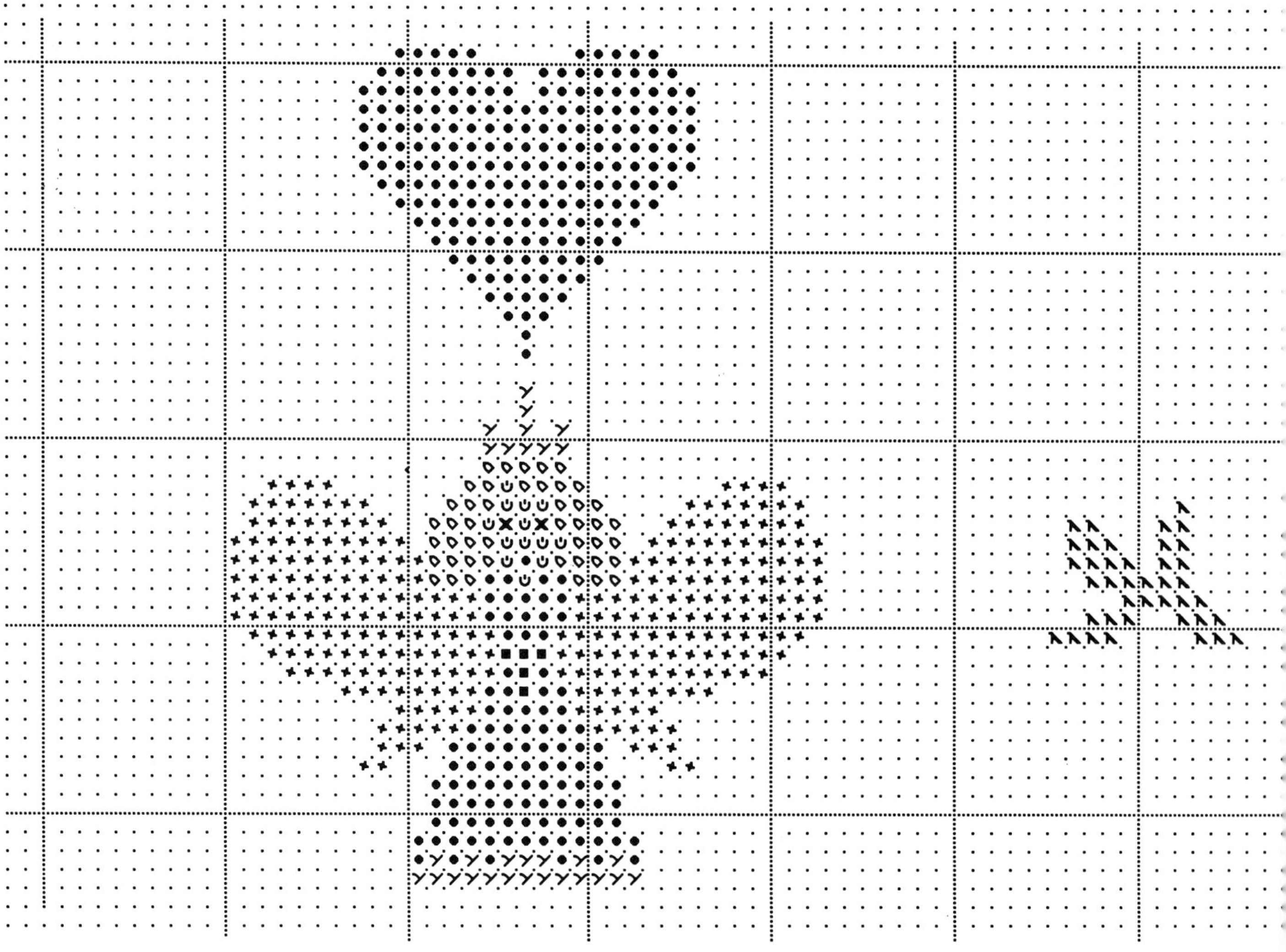

OLD-FASHIONED CHRISTMAS KITCHEN

● *A bit of nostalgia for you to embroider. A wood stove, food for the Christmas table, and a contented kitty . . . all recall memories of past Christmases. This little picture is very simple to make, and it can stay on your wall throughout the year.*

**OLD-FASHIONED
CHRISTMAS KITCHEN**

Cut size: 12″ × 14″
Finished size: 8″ × 10″

#18 even-weave linen
  4 strands of floss

	DMC#	
••••••	349	red
◊◊◊◊◊◊	922	copper
▽▽▽▽▽▽	783	gold ochre
┗┙┗┙┗┙	400	chestnut
×××××	823	deep ultramarine blue
٩٩٩٩٩٩	415	dove grey
ʟʟʟʟʟʟ	989	med. olive
ʌʌʌʌʌʌ	701	med. green
ʏʏʏʏʏʏ	973	med. yellow
ѵѵѵѵѵѵ	907	chartreuse
✦✦✦✦✦✦		white

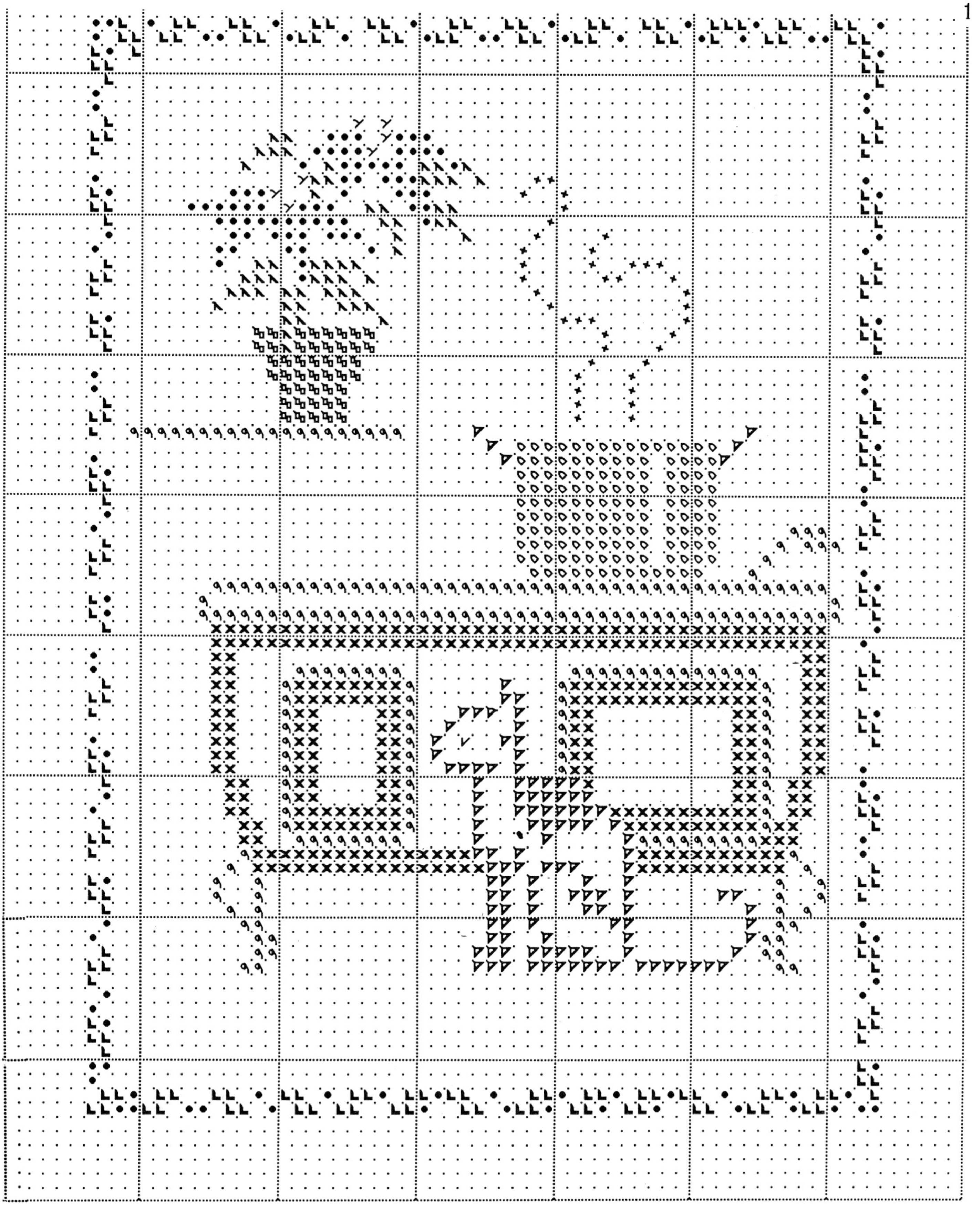

TWELVE DAYS OF CHRISTMAS

● *This is one of the most elaborate and ambitious projects in the book, well worth the time and effort required to complete it. I really enjoyed designing and making this piece—it's one of my favorites.*

TWELVE DAYS OF CHRISTMAS

Cut size: 20″ × 20″
Finished size: 16″ × 16″

#18 even-weave linen
  4 strands of floss
  4 yd. gold metallic thread

	DMC#	
● ● ● ● ●	349	red
⁄ ⁄ ⁄ ⁄ ⁄	321	scarlet
● ● ● ● ●	600	dk. rose
○ ○ ○ ○ ○	602	dk. pink
ʊ ʊ ʊ ʊ ʊ	818	med. pink
◇ ◇ ◇ ◇ ◇	948	flesh
ʊ ʊ ʊ ʊ ʊ	891	strawberry
○ ○ ○ ○ ○	894	lt. strawberry
⋎ ⋎ ⋎ ⋎ ⋎	971	lt. orange
⋎ ⋎ ⋎ ⋎ ⋎	973	med. yellow
⋎ ⋎ ⋎ ⋎ ⋎	307	lt. yellow
× × × × ×	725	gold
⋎ ⋎ ⋎ ⋎ ⋎	782	bronze

▽ ▽ ▽ ▽ ▽	783	gold ochre
ꙅ ꙅ ꙅ ꙅ ꙅ	434	coffee
⸌ ⸌ ⸌ ⸌ ⸌	436	cafe au lait
⋎ ⋎ ⋎ ⋎ ⋎	840	dusty brown
◣ ◣ ◣ ◣ ◣	839	dk. dusty brown
⁄ ⁄ ⁄ ⁄ ⁄	842	tan
٩ ٩ ٩ ٩ ٩	415	dove grey
◀ ◀ ◀ ◀ ◀	318	med. grey
⌐ ⌐ ⌐ ⌐ ⌐	413	charcoal grey
◣ ◣ ◣ ◣ ◣	3346	dk. olive
▲ ▲ ▲ ▲ ▲	699	dk. green
⋁ ⋁ ⋁ ⋁ ⋁	907	chartreuse
■ ■ ■ ■ ■	827	lt. blue

□ □ □ □ □	799	med. blue
× × × × ×	823	deep ultramar blue
ʊ ʊ ʊ ʊ ʊ	996	sky blue
⊠ ⊠ ⊠ ⊠ ⊠	718	med. red viol
✦ ✦ ✦ ✦ ✦		white
✧ ✧ ✧ ✧ ✧		gold metallic
⁙ ⁙ ⁙ ⁙ ⁙		natural (ecru)
	782	bronze backst
----------	823	deep ultramar blue backsti
————		

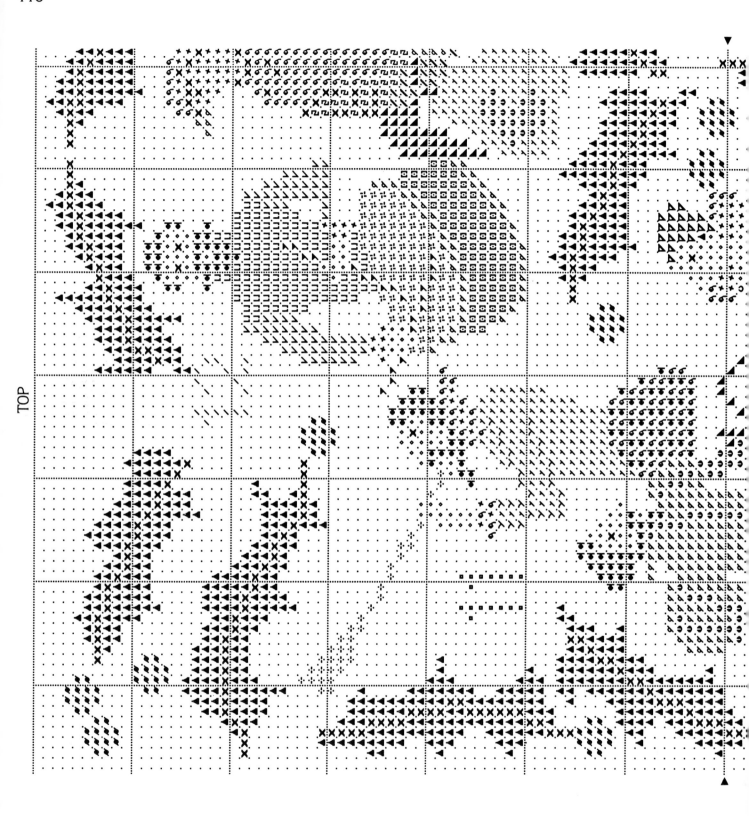

BOTTOM

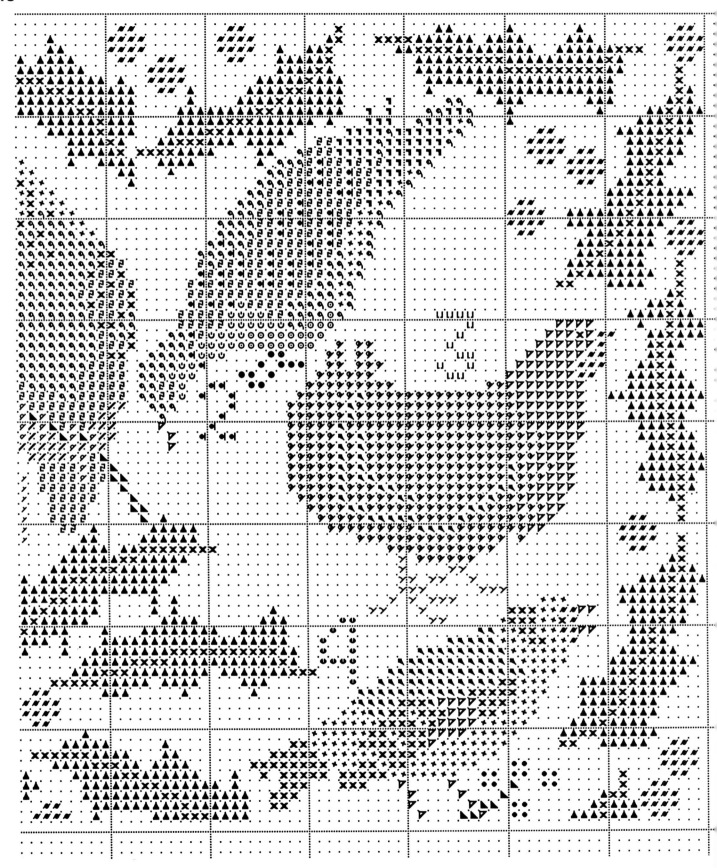

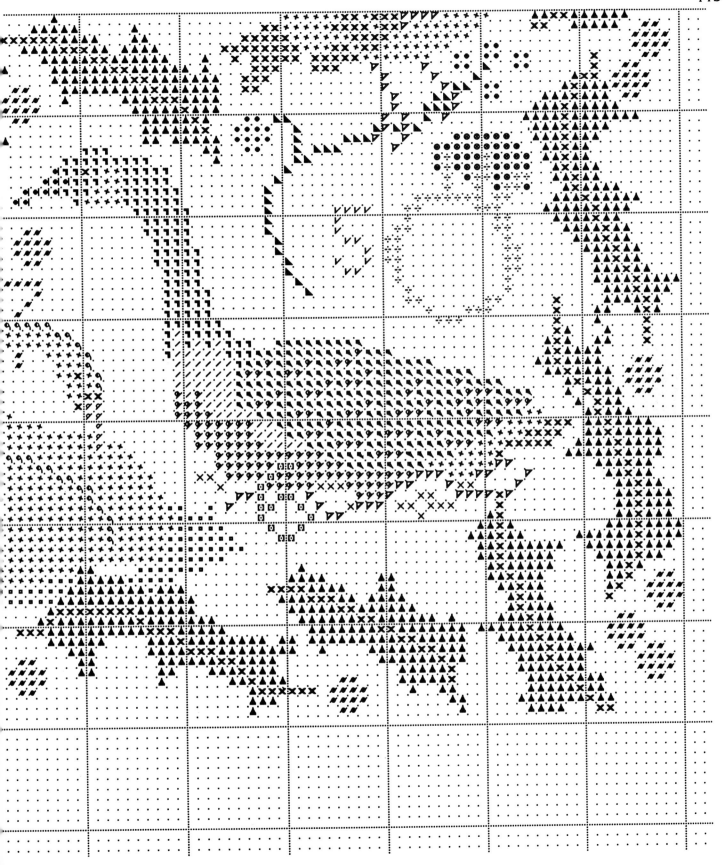

NATIVITY SCENE

● *A very simple and serene nativity scene. So quick and easy, it could be made in a weekend. This charming piece will bring the quiet, graceful spirit of Christmas into your home.*

NATIVITY SCENE

Cut size: 14″ × 16″
Finished size: 10″ × 12″

#14 Aida cloth
  4 strands of floss, stitched over 2″ × 2″
  2 yd. gold metallic thread

           DMC#
××××× 725 gold
✧✧✧✧✧   gold metallic

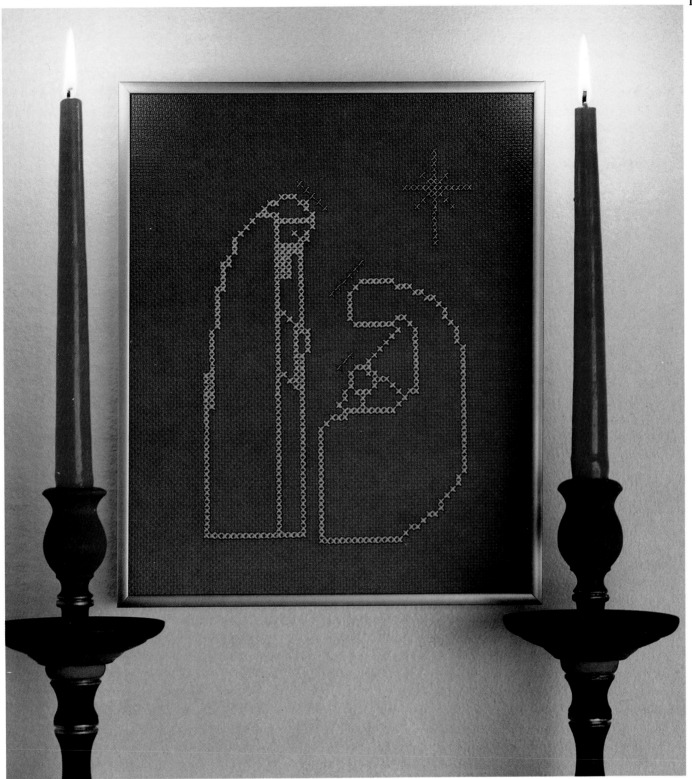

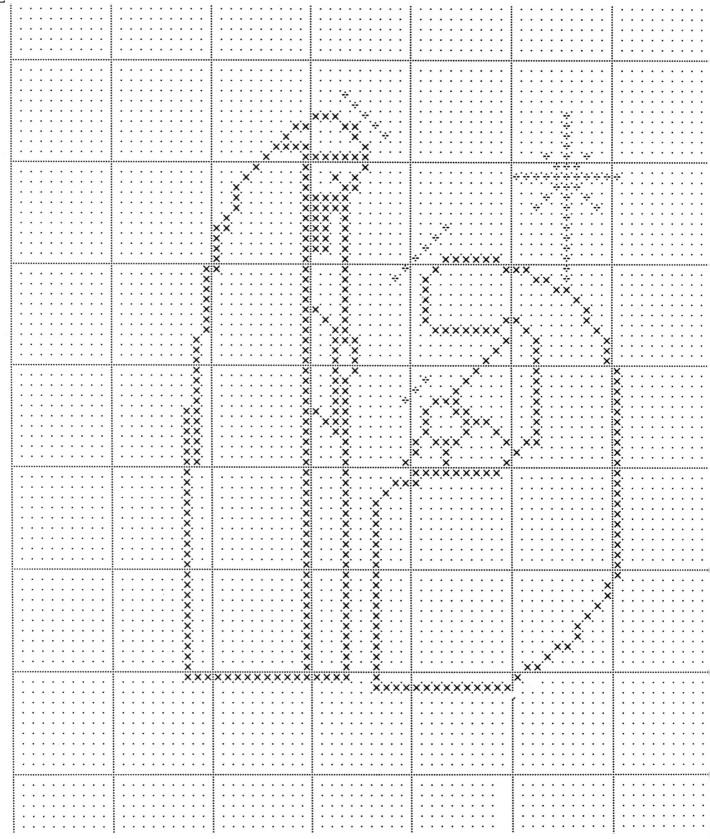

SANTA'S WORKSHOP

● *Don't be discouraged by the elaborateness of this project. It is worth every hour of stitching and changing color. The piece is fun and full of activity and preparation. Santa's reindeer looks ready to make everyone smile.*

SANTA'S WORKSHOP

Cut size: 20″ × 26″
Finished size: 16″ × 22″

#18 even-weave linen
  4 strands of floss
  2 yd. gold metallic thread

DMC#

Symbol	#	Color
●●●●●	349	red
◢◢◢◢◢	321	scarlet
◡◡◡◡◡	818	med. pink
○○○○○	894	lt. strawberry
◡◡◡◡◡	891	strawberry
ʏʏʏʏʏ	3708	pale yellow
⅄⅄⅄⅄⅄	973	med. yellow
×××××	725	gold
⅄⅄⅄⅄⅄	782	bronze
✗✗✗✗✗	433	chocolate
ƨƨƨƨƨ	434	coffee
∕∕∕∕∕	436	cafe au lait
⅄⅄⅄⅄⅄	840	dusty brown
◣◣◣◣◣	839	dk. dusty brown
/////	842	tan
٩٩٩٩٩	415	dove grey
◁◁◁◁◁	318	med. grey
¶¶¶¶¶	413	charcoal grey
◤◤◤◤◤	3346	dk. olive
ᴠᴠᴠᴠᴠ	907	chartreuse
◘◘◘◘◘	912	emerald
▪▪▪▪▪	827	lt. blue
×××××	823	deep ultramarine blue
▪▪▪▪▪	322	dk. grey-blue
ᴜᴜᴜᴜᴜ	996	sky blue
◆◆◆◆◆	208	lilac
✦✦✦✦✦		white
✧✧✧✧✧		gold metallic
⁓⁓⁓⁓⁓		ecru (natural)
———	823	deep ultramarine blue backstitch
-----	415	dove grey backstitch

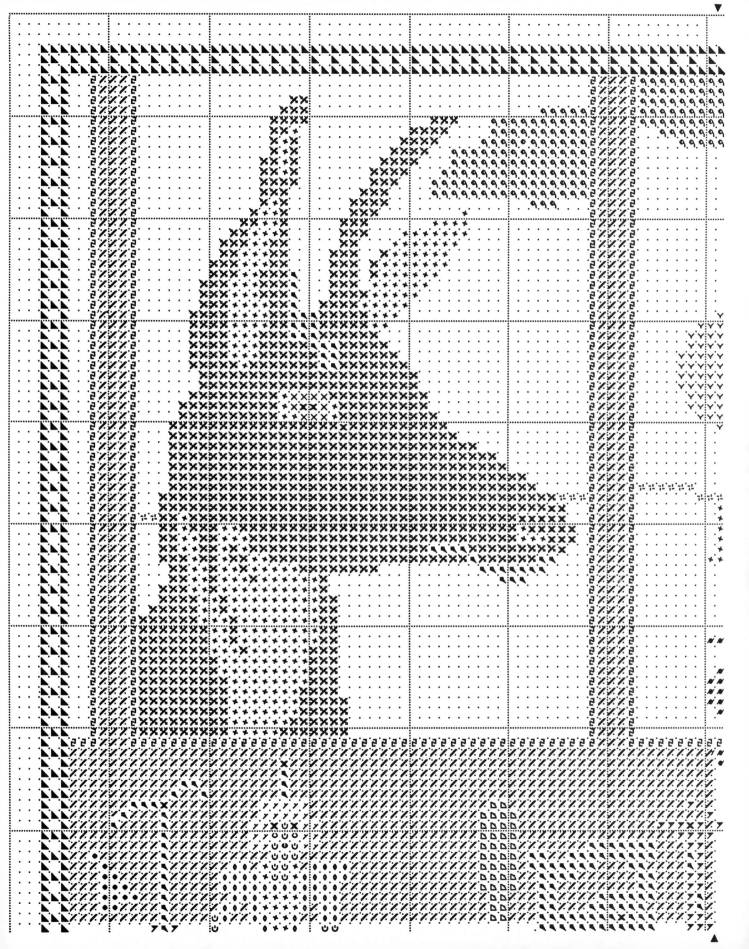

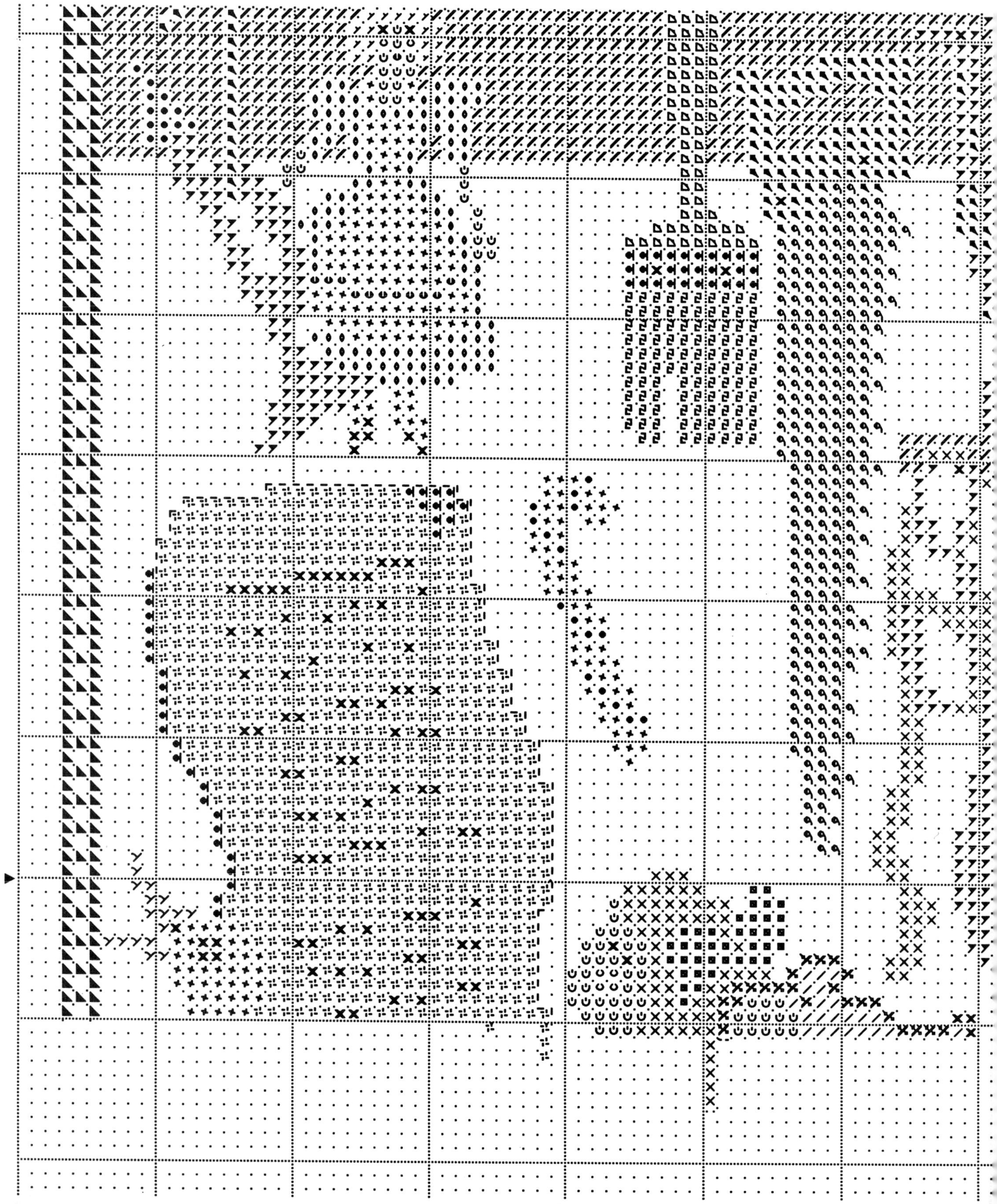

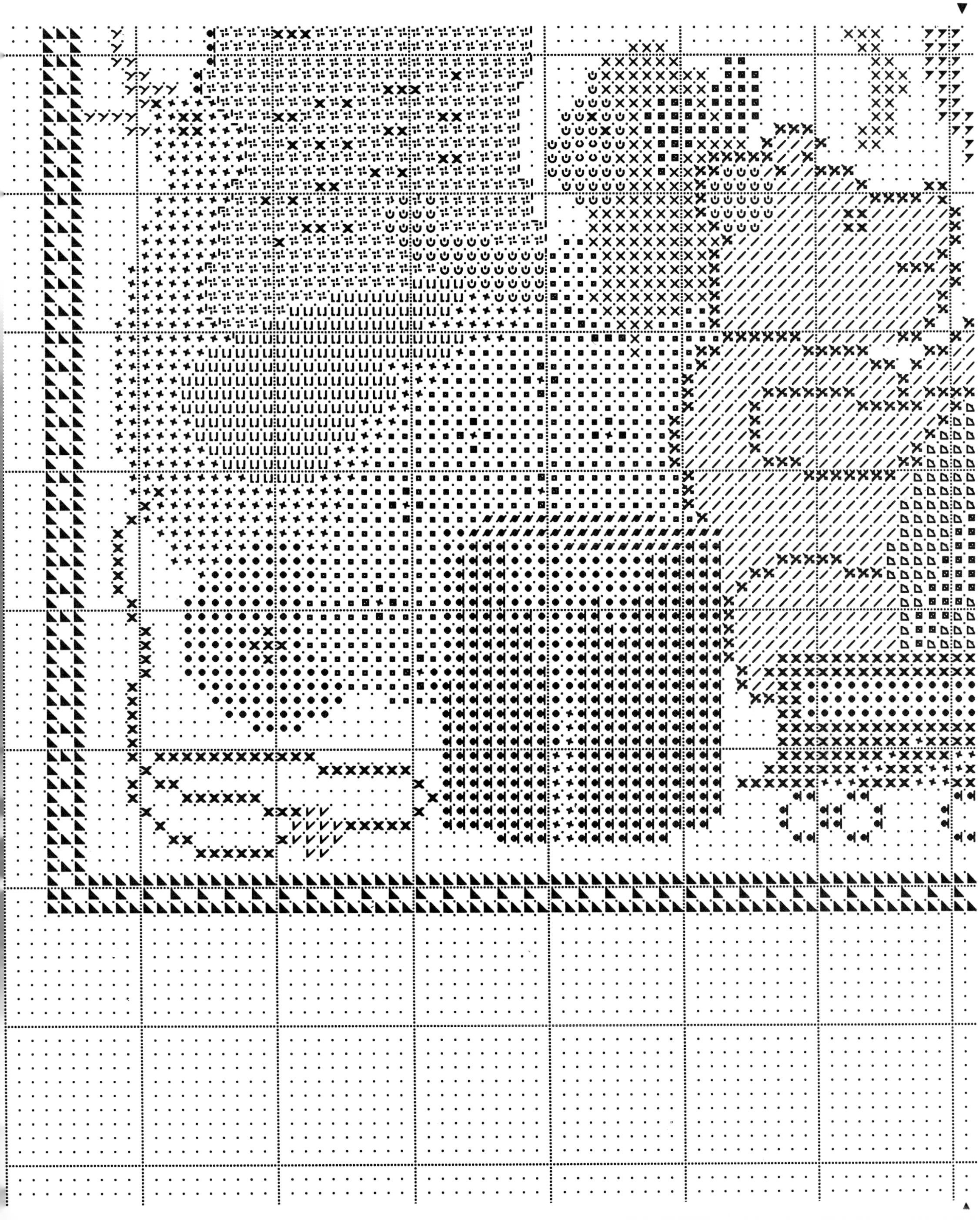

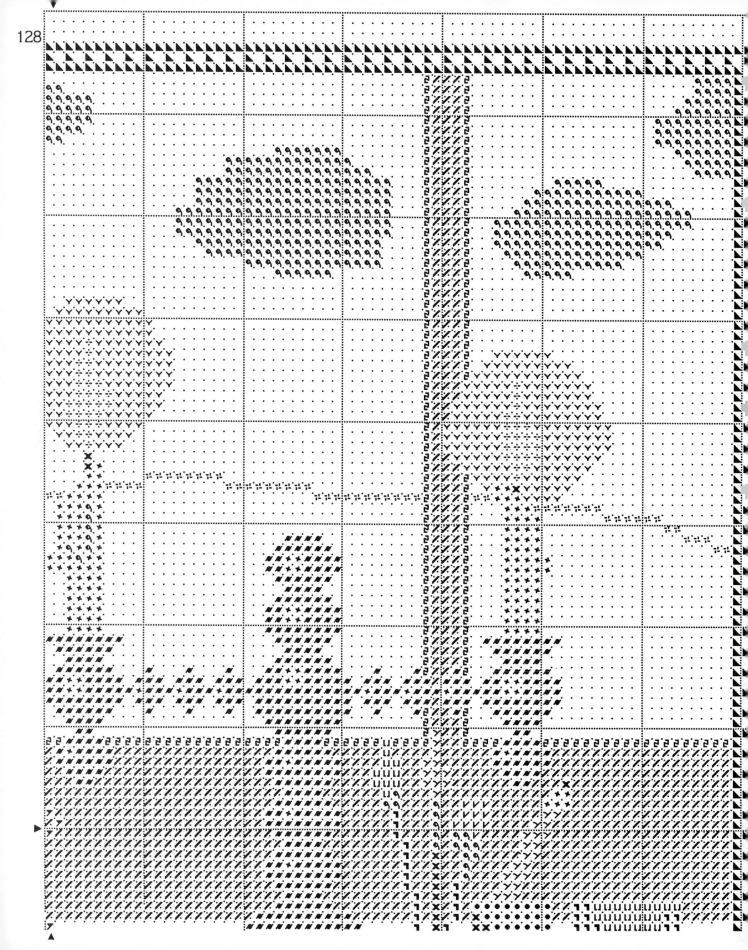

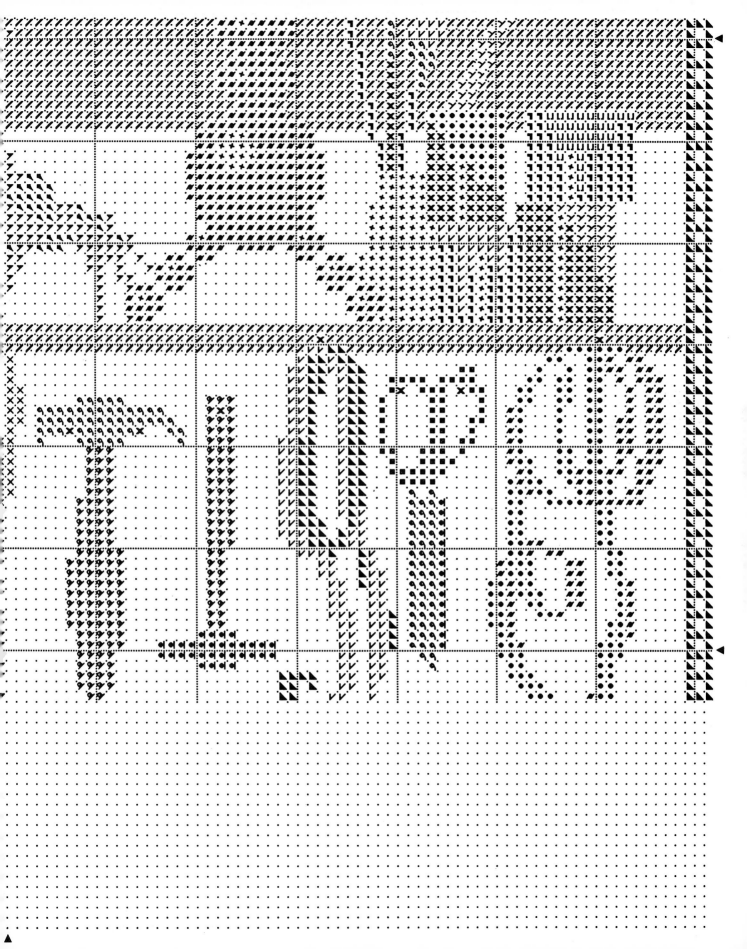

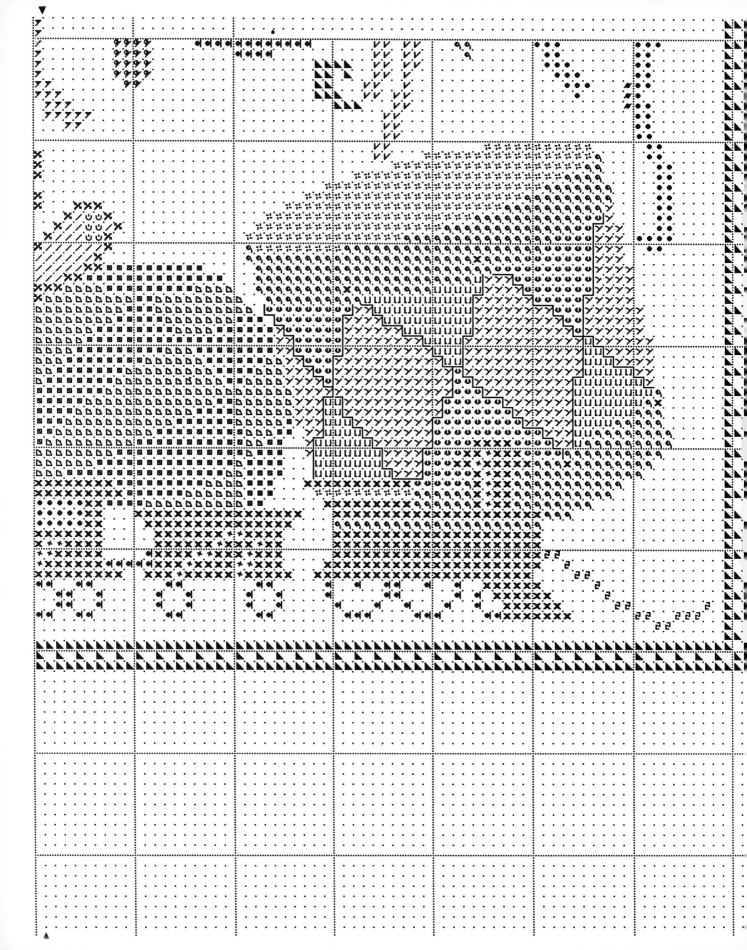

CRÊCHE

● *We designed this crêche with a folk-art feeling. The piece is simple and direct, with deep, rich colors.*

The beautiful symmetry and lovely motifs announce the Christmas season in all its glorious wonder. This framed picture would be inspiring in any room.

CRÊCHE

Cut size: 18″ × 16″
Finished size: 14″ × 12″

#18 even-weave linen
  4 strands of floss
  8 yd. gold metallic thread

	DMC#	
✗✗✗✗✗	321	scarlet
◇◇◇◇◇◇	948	flesh
✗✗✗✗✗✗	725	gold
╱╱╱╱╱╱	436	cafe au lait
◆◆◆◆◆◆	840	dusty brown
✗✗✗✗✗	823	deep ultramarine blue
◀◀◀◀◀◀	318	med. grey
٩٩٩٩٩٩	415	dove grey
⋀⋀⋀⋀⋀⋀	701	med. green
◻◻◻◻◻◻	799	med. blue
■■■■■■	824	dark blue
+++++		white
✧✧✧✧✧✧		gold metallic
——————	823	deep ultramarine blue backstitch
●●●●●●	208	lilac

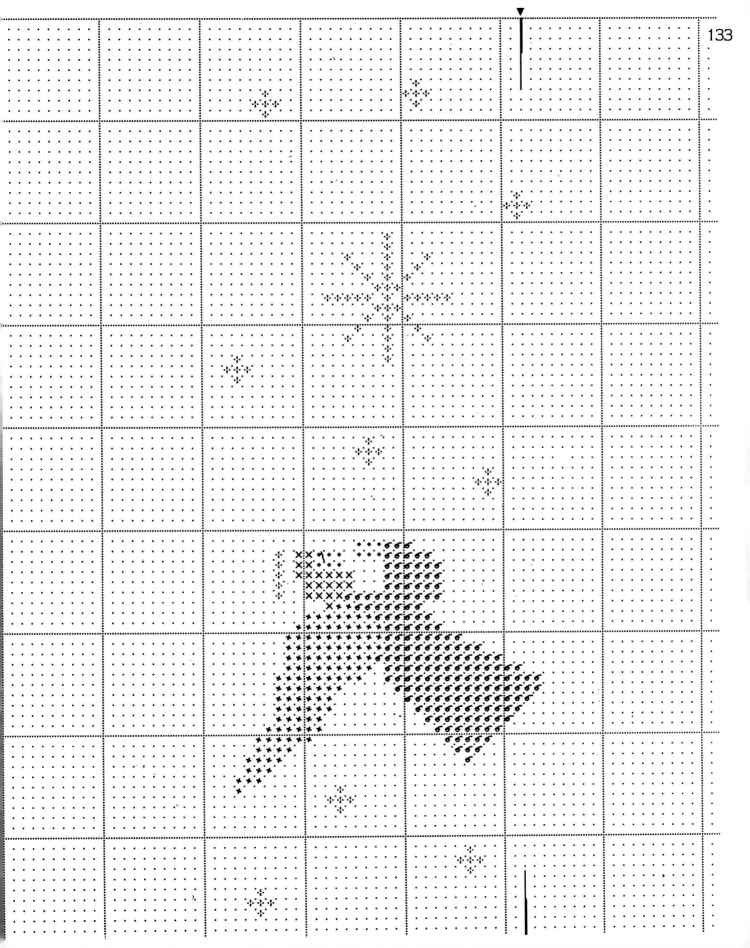

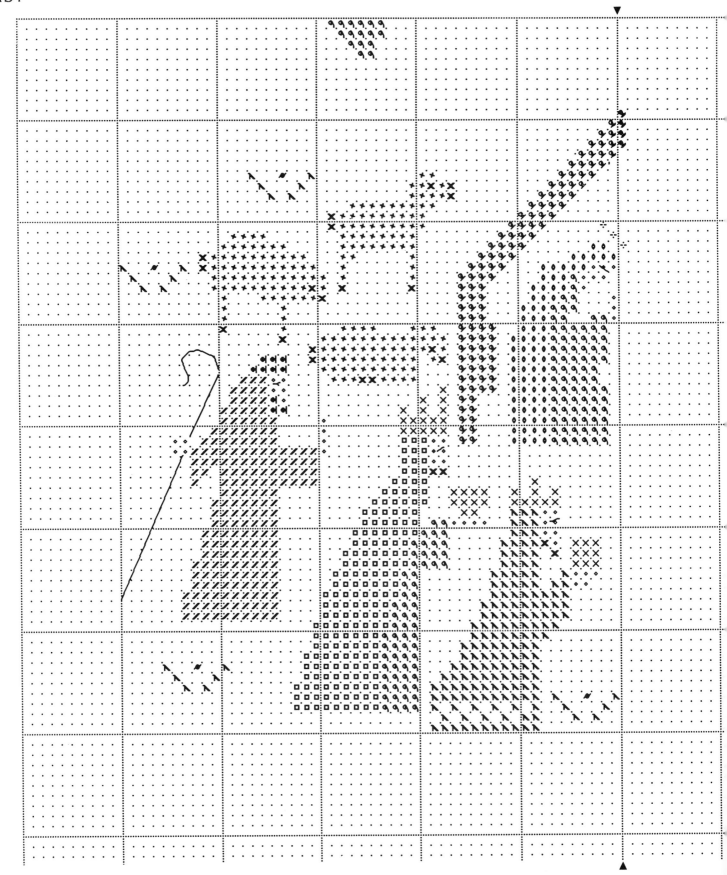

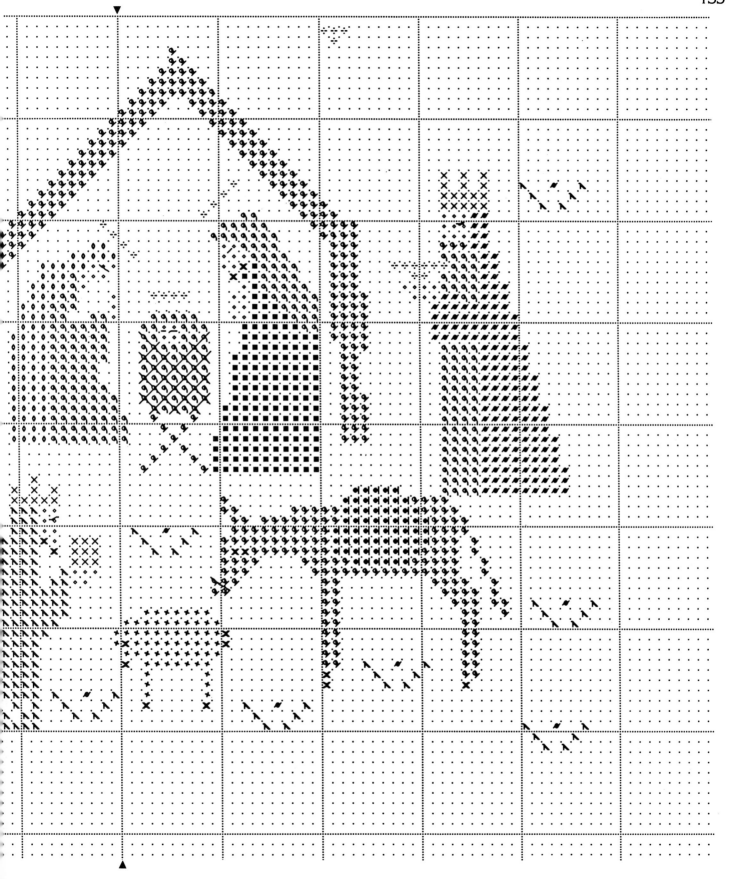

Deck the House

PINE CONE STUFFED WREATH

● *A simple and decorative wreath. Picture it on your living room door, or even on a window. The pine cone is a traditional symbol that has been used throughout the ages as a decorative motif. Your family and friends will enjoy this bright, colorful wreath.*

PINE CONE STUFFED WREATH

Cut size: 12″ × 12″
Finished size: 8″ × 8″

#12 Aida cloth
  4 strands of floss

	DMC#	
᧒᧒᧒᧒᧒᧒	400	chestnut
▲▲▲▲▲▲	3346	dk. olive
ʟʟʟʟʟʟ	989	med. olive

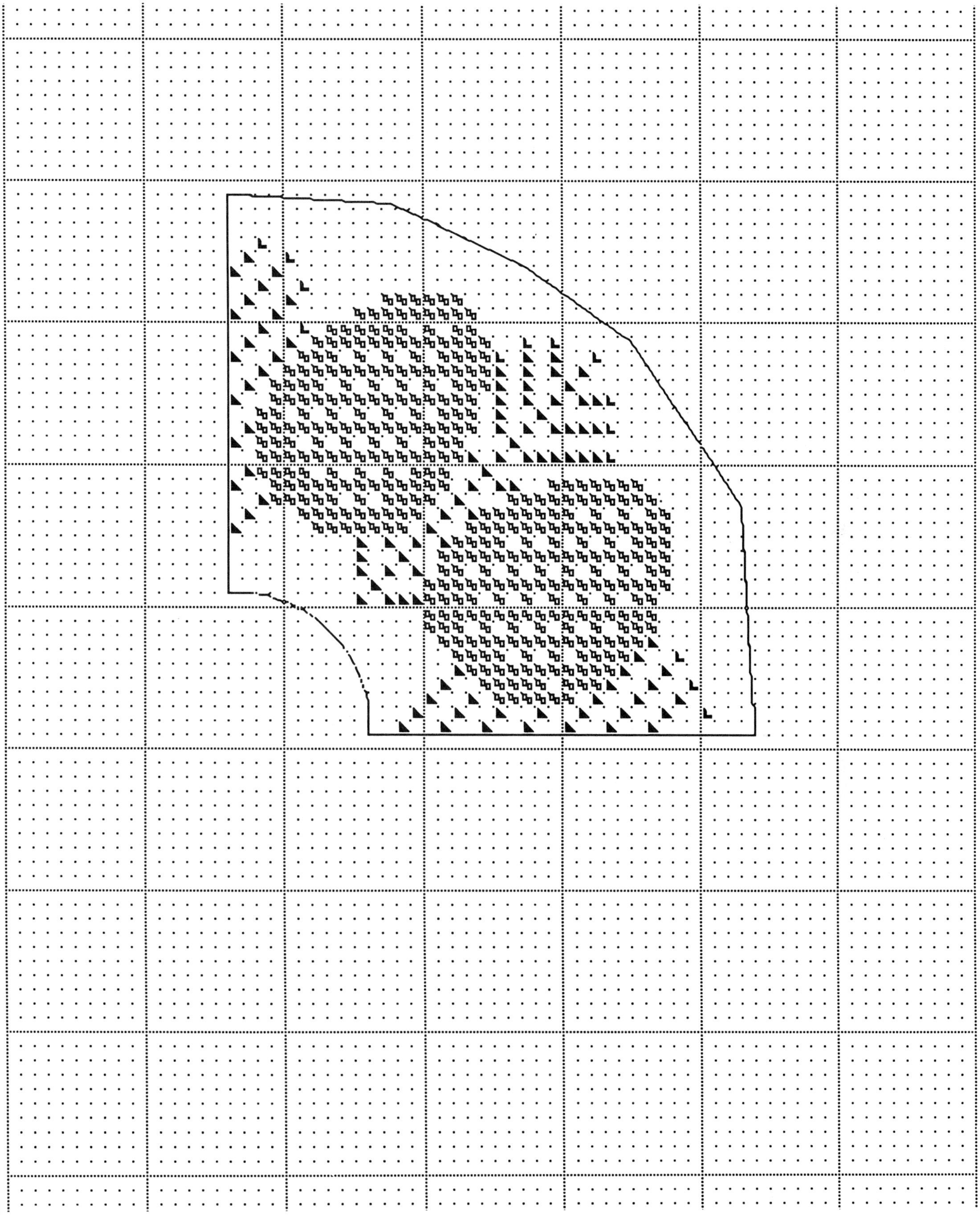

SANTA STUFFED WREATH

● *We made this wreath quite large. It would be suitable on a front door (weather conditions permitting), or in an entryway. Evergreens or pine cones can be placed in the center. This impressive wreath makes a bold statement, wherever it is placed.*

SANTA STUFFED WREATH

Cut size: 22″ × 22″
Finished size: 18″ in diameter

#12 Aida cloth
  3 strands of floss
  1½ yd. ruffle

	DMC#	
• • • • •	349	red
◇ ◇ ◇ ◇ ◇	948	flesh
ʏʏʏʏʏʏ	973	med. yellow
×××××	823	deep ultramarine blue
ʌʌʌʌʌʌ	701	med. green
+ + + + +		white
———	415	dove grey backstitch
··········	823	deep ultramarine blue backstitch

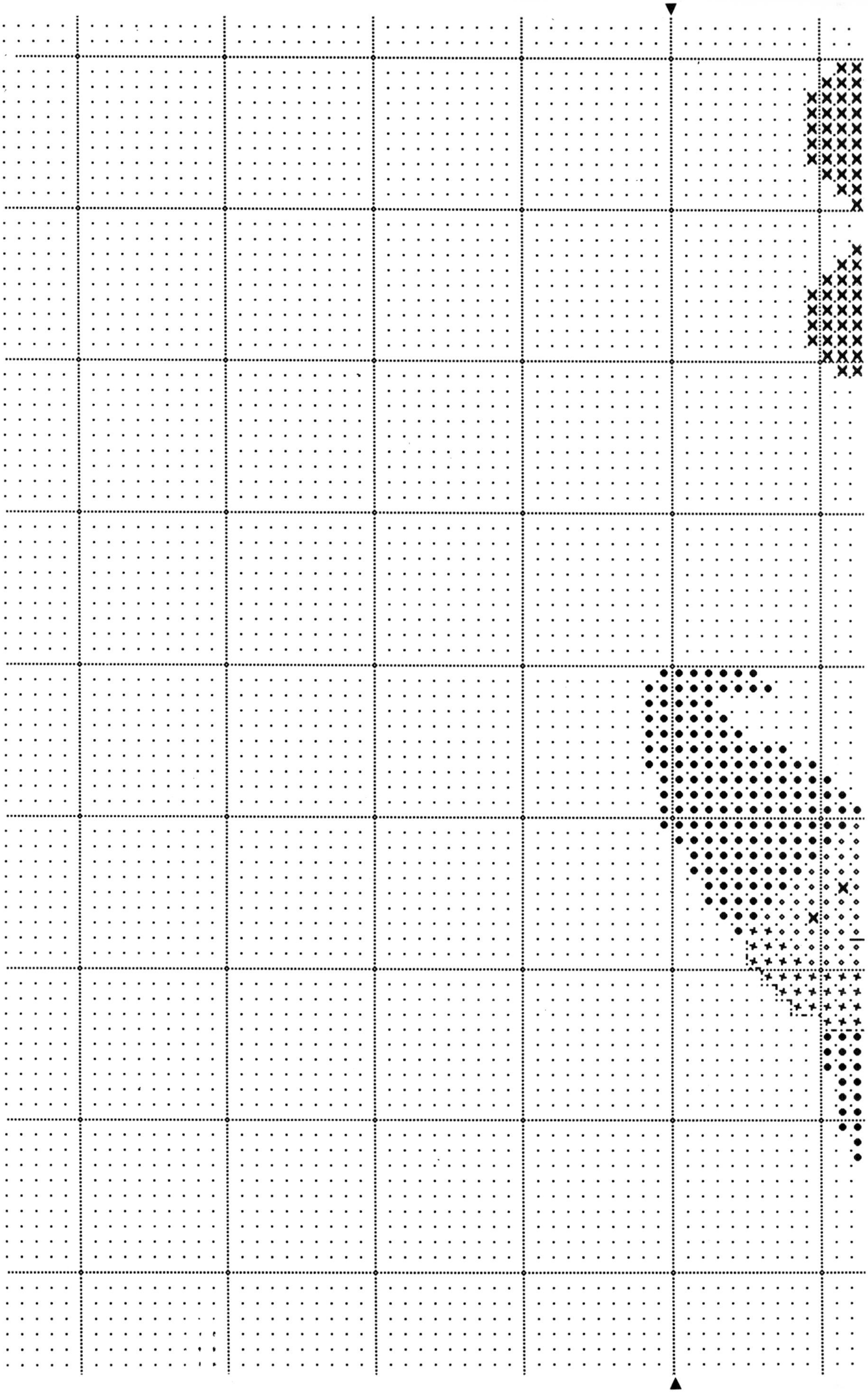

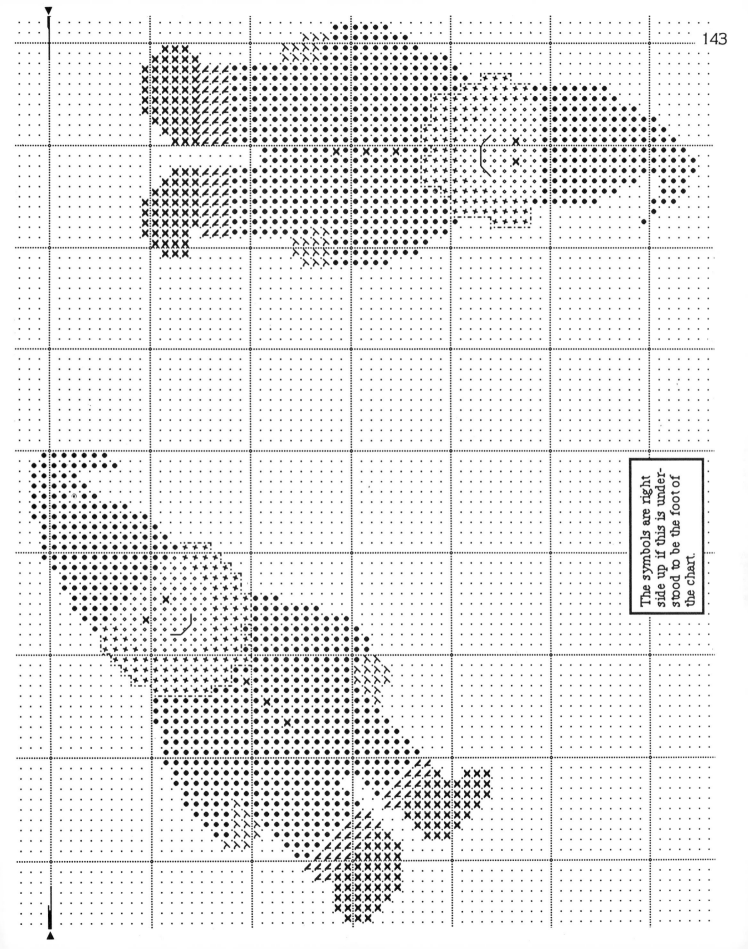

143

The symbols are right side up if this is understood to be the foot of the chart.

144

CANDY CANE STUFFED WREATH

• *You can never have too many wreaths in your "Christmas home." Personally, I like them on most of my doors. The candy canes and holly are such fun to cross-stitch, you may even want to make two wreaths.*

CANDY CANE STUFFED WREATH

Cut size: 12″ × 12″
Finished size: 8″ × 8″

#12 Aida cloth
 4 strands of floss

	DMC#	
• • • • •	349	red
✔✔✔✔✔	321	scarlet
ʌʌʌʌʌ	701	med. green
× × × × ×		silver metallic

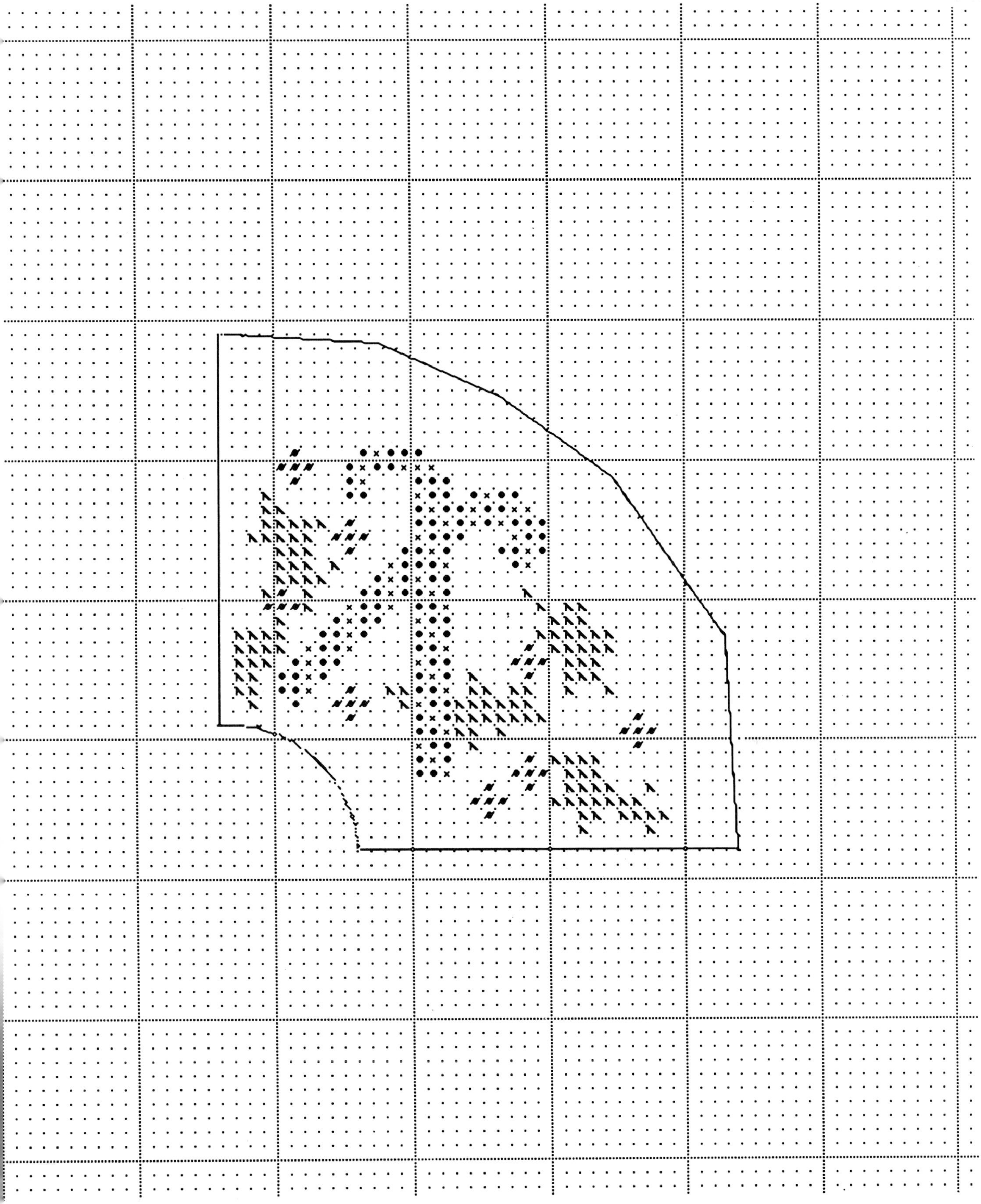

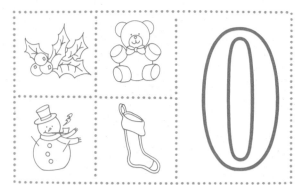

OLD-FASHIONED CHRISTMAS CARD HOLDER

● *Hang this well-designed and func-tional card holder by the front door or mantel. It's a neat, decorative way to keep your Christmas cards together, and it's quick and easy to make. Keep in mind that the material is cut in one piece, so you must fold up the pouch before you start to stitch.*

**OLD-FASHIONED
CHRISTMAS CARD HOLDER**

Cut size: 24″ × 14″
Finished size: 16″ × 10″

#12 Aida cloth
  4 strands of floss

	DMC#	
• • • • •	349	red
✔✔✔✔✔	321	scarlet
◉◉◉◉◉	602	dk. pink
◇ ◇ ◇ ◇ ◇	948	flesh
↳↳↳↳↳	400	chestnut
✗✗✗✗✗	433	chocolate
× × × × ×	725	gold
ʟʟʟʟʟ	989	med. olive
✔✔✔✔✔	907	chartreuse
✗✗✗✗✗	823	deep ultramarine
+ + + + +		blue
× × × ×		silver metallic
——————	823	deep ultramarine blue backstitch

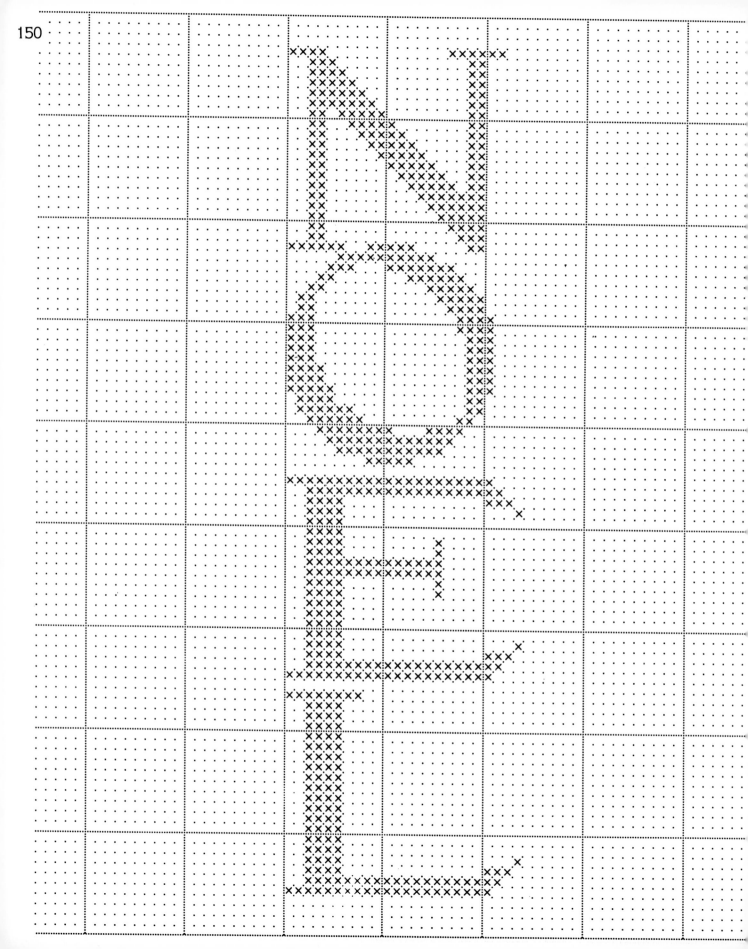

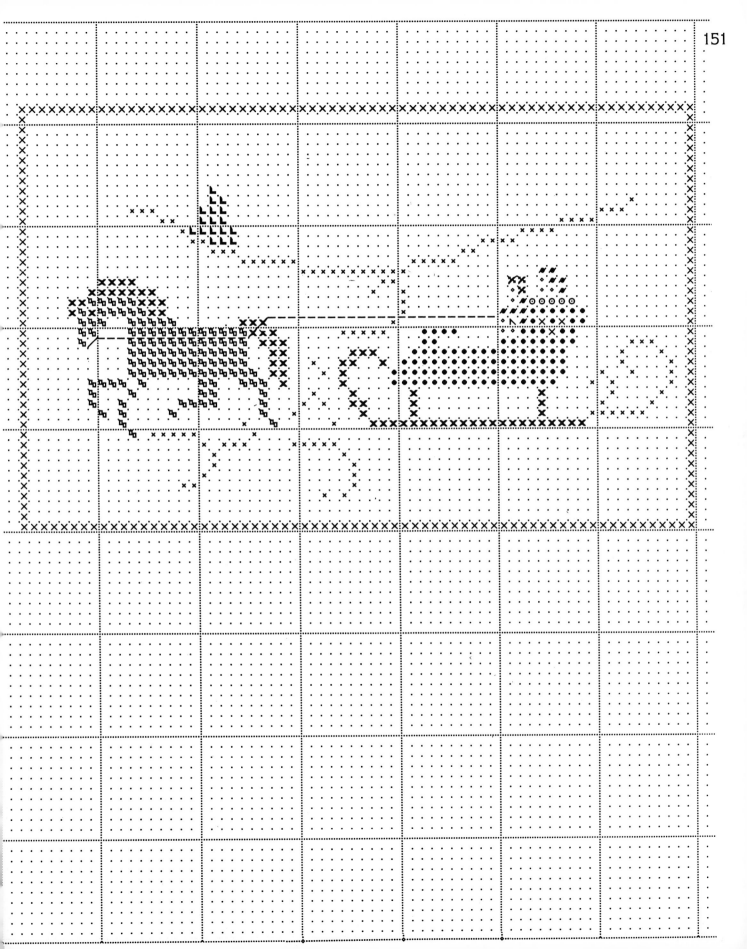

ANGEL GUEST TOWEL AND

CHRISTMAS WREATH GUEST TOWEL

● *Two very easy projects that will add a special festive touch to your bathroom. They also make wonderful gifts. If you like, you can personalize them. (See Alphabet, page 187.)*

ANGEL GUEST TOWEL

Cut size: 14″ × 18″
Finished size: 10″ × 14″

#12 Aida cloth
  3 strands of floss

       DMC#
×××××× 725 gold
●●●●● 349 red
○○○○○○ 819 pink

CHRISTMAS WREATH GUEST TOWEL

Cut size: 14″ × 18″
Finished size: 10″ × 14″

#12 Aida cloth
  3 strands of floss

       DMC#
●●●●● 349 red
✗✗✗✗✗ 321 scarlet
ʌʌʌʌʌ 701 med. green

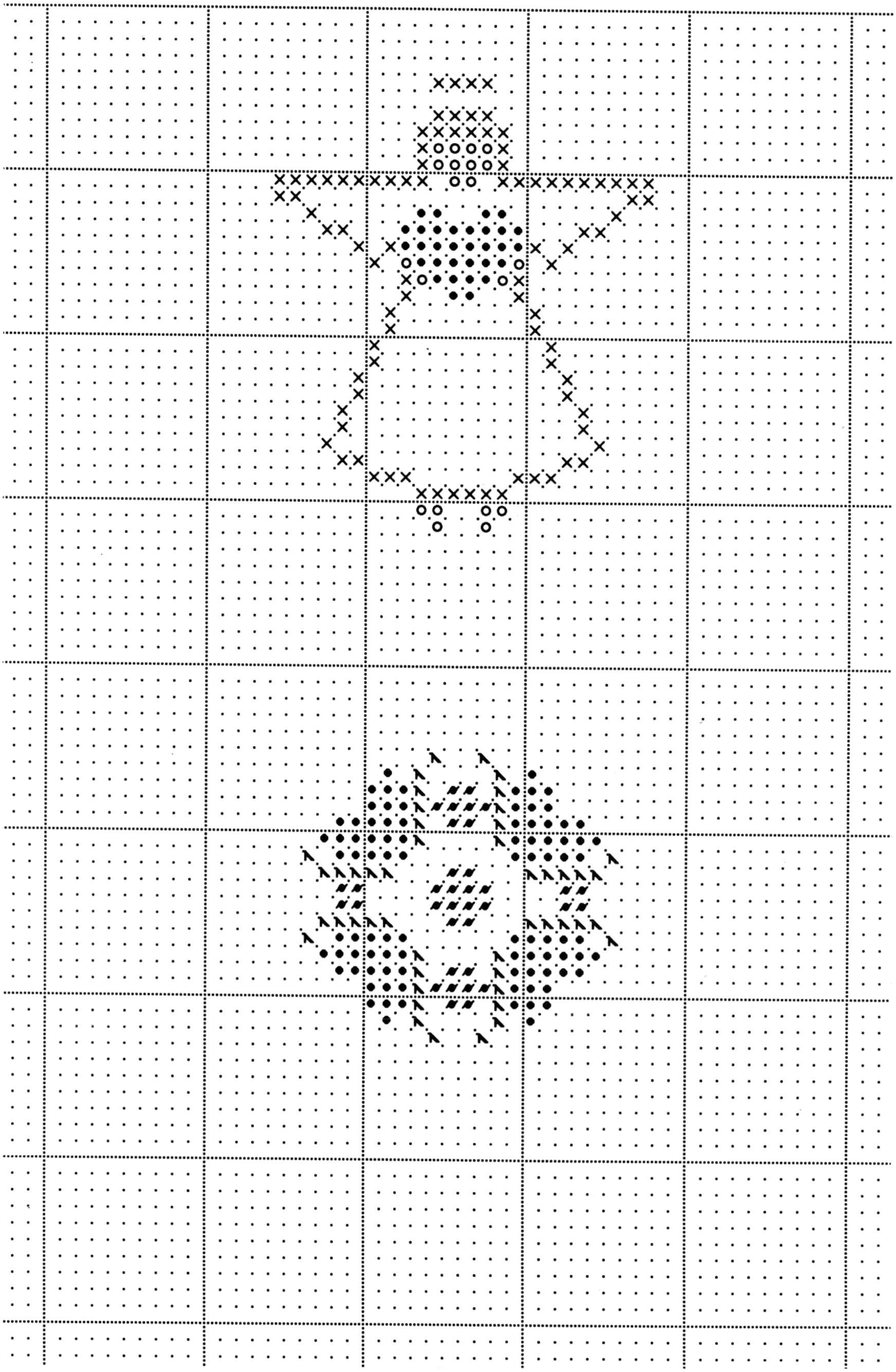

BLUE PEACE DOVE PILLOW

● The dove . . . a universal symbol of peace and love. This is a year-round design. Very easy to make—it's an evening's project. And it would make a wonderful gift.

BLUE PEACE DOVE PILLOW

Cut size: 14″ × 14″
Finished size: 9″ × 10″

#14 Aida cloth
  4 strands of floss, stitched over 2″ × 2″

       DMC#
⊙⊙⊙⊙⊙⊙ 602 dk. pink
✶✶✶✶✶   white

SNOWFLAKE PILLOW

Cut size: 14″ × 14″
Finished size: 10″ × 10″

#14 Aida cloth
  2 strands of floss

       DMC#
✶✶✶✶✶   white

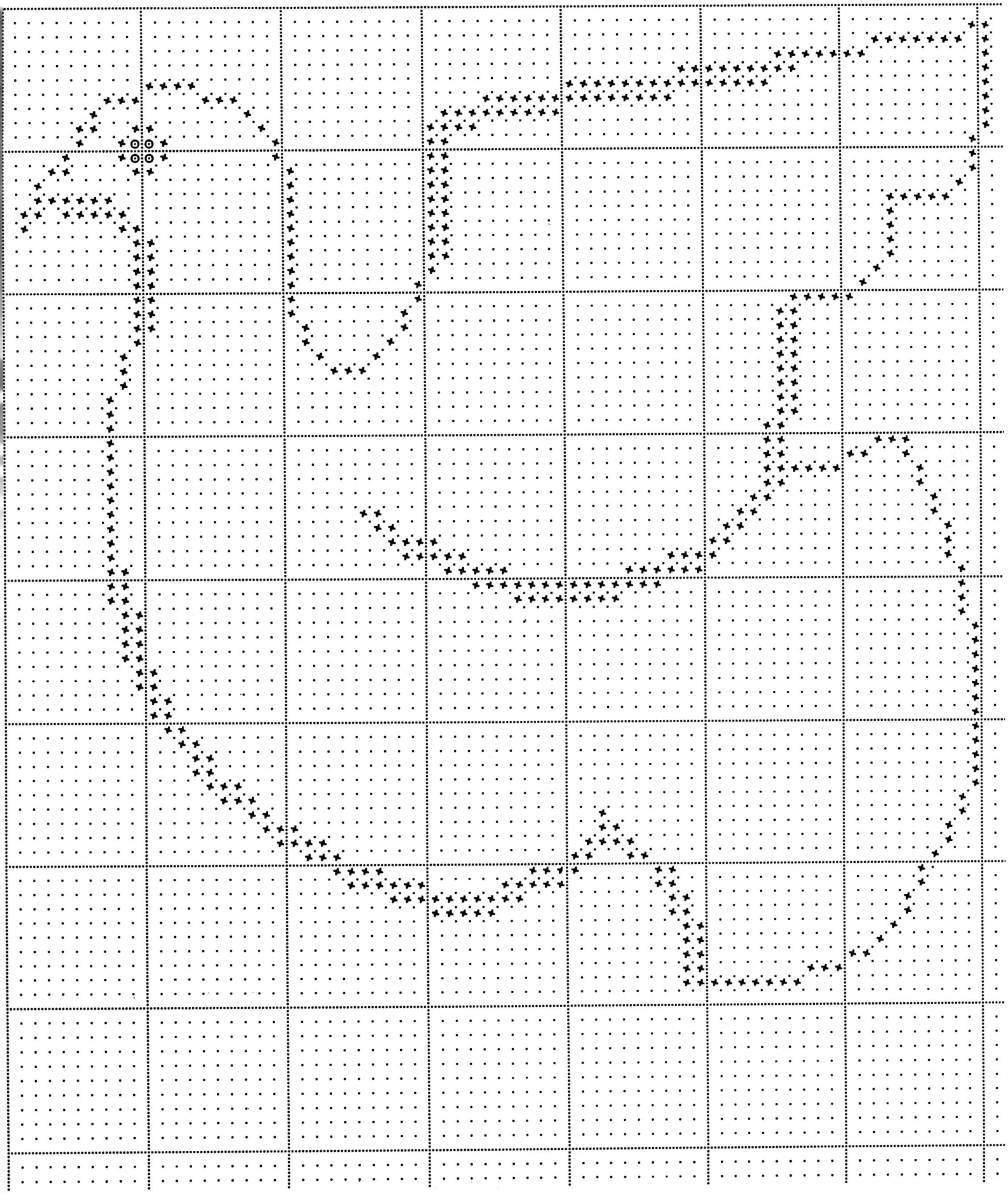

SNOWFLAKE PILLOW

● *A snowflake can take many different shapes and forms. We liked this one because it's so eye-catching. The design is also suitable for a wall hanging or a picture.*

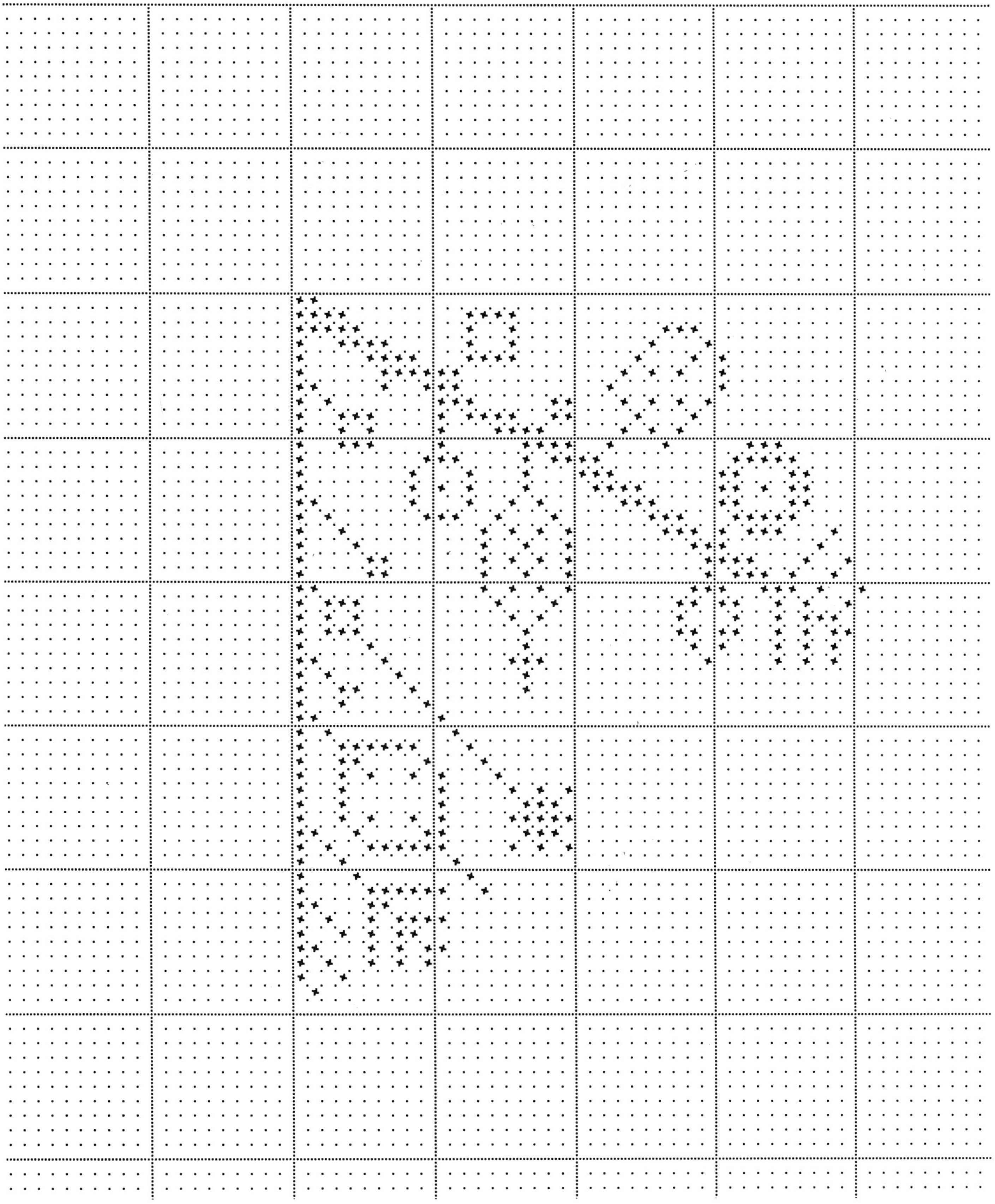

CHRISTMAS PIG PILLOW

● *HO HO HO! This happy little pig is a joy to make. Put the finished pillow anywhere in your home—living room, dining room, bedroom or child's room. Its good humor will brighten the Christmas season, and all the days after.*

CHRISTMAS PIG PILLOW

Cut size: 14″ × 12″
Finished size: 9½″ × 7½″

#18 even weave linen
  4 strands of floss
  1 yd. gold metallic thread

	DMC#	
• • • • • •	349	red
ʊ ʊ ʊ ʊ ʊ ʊ	818	med. pink
o o o o o o	819	pink
ʏ ʏ ʏ ʏ ʏ	307	lt. yellow
✗ ✗ ✗ ✗ ✗ ✗	433	chocolate brown
⁊ ⁊ ⁊ ⁊ ⁊ ⁊	436	cafe au lait
✗ ✗ ✗ ✗ ✗	823	deep ultramarine blue
ʟ ʟ ʟ ʟ ʟ ʟ	989	med. olive
■ ■ ■ ■ ■ ■	824	dk. blue
◉ ◉ ◉ ◉ ◉ ◉	915	dk. red violet
✧ ✧ ✧ ✧ ✧ ✧		gold metallic

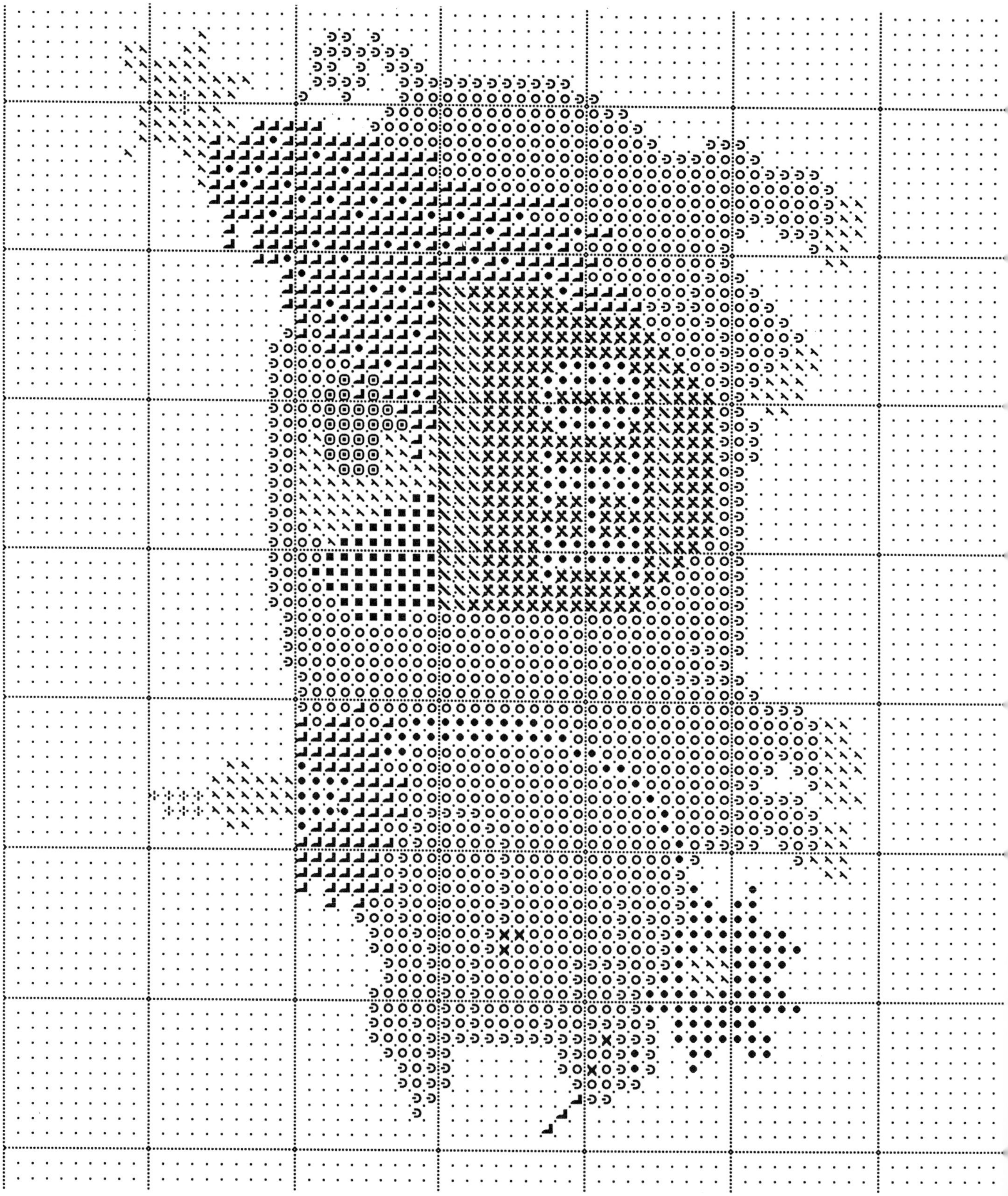

DANCING GNOMES PILLOW

● Merry gnomes dancing around the Christmas tree! Make room for these friendly creatures. Their antics will uplift your spirits, and bring you joy.

A fun project that can also be made as a wall hanging.

DANCING GNOMES PILLOW

Cut size: 12″ × 12″
Finished size: 8″ × 8″

#12 Aida cloth
  3 strands of floss

	DMC#	
● ● ● ● ●	349	red
⁄ ⁄ ⁄ ⁄ ⁄	321	scarlet
× × × × ×	725	gold
ⅎ ⅎ ⅎ ⅎ ⅎ	400	chestnut
• • • • •	948	flesh
ʌ ʌ ʌ ʌ ʌ	701	med. green
▲ ▲ ▲ ▲ ▲	3346	dk. olive
× × × × ×	823	deep ultramarine blue
× × × ×		silver metallic

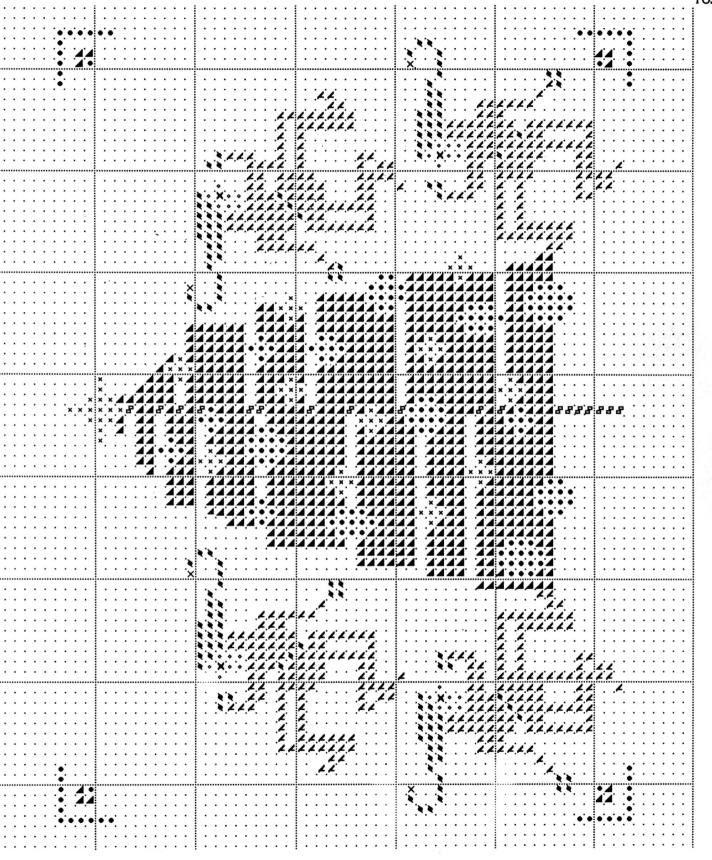

POINSETTIA PILLOW

● *This poinsettia will bloom year after year in your home—no watering necessary! The gentle, graceful design will complement any decor, and will brighten the darkest corner. It's easy and fast to make.*

POINSETTIA PILLOW

Cut size: 12″ × 12″
Finished size: 8″ × 8″

#12 Aida cloth
  3 strands of floss

            DMC#
●●●●●● 349 red
ʏʏʏʏʏʏ 973 med. yellow

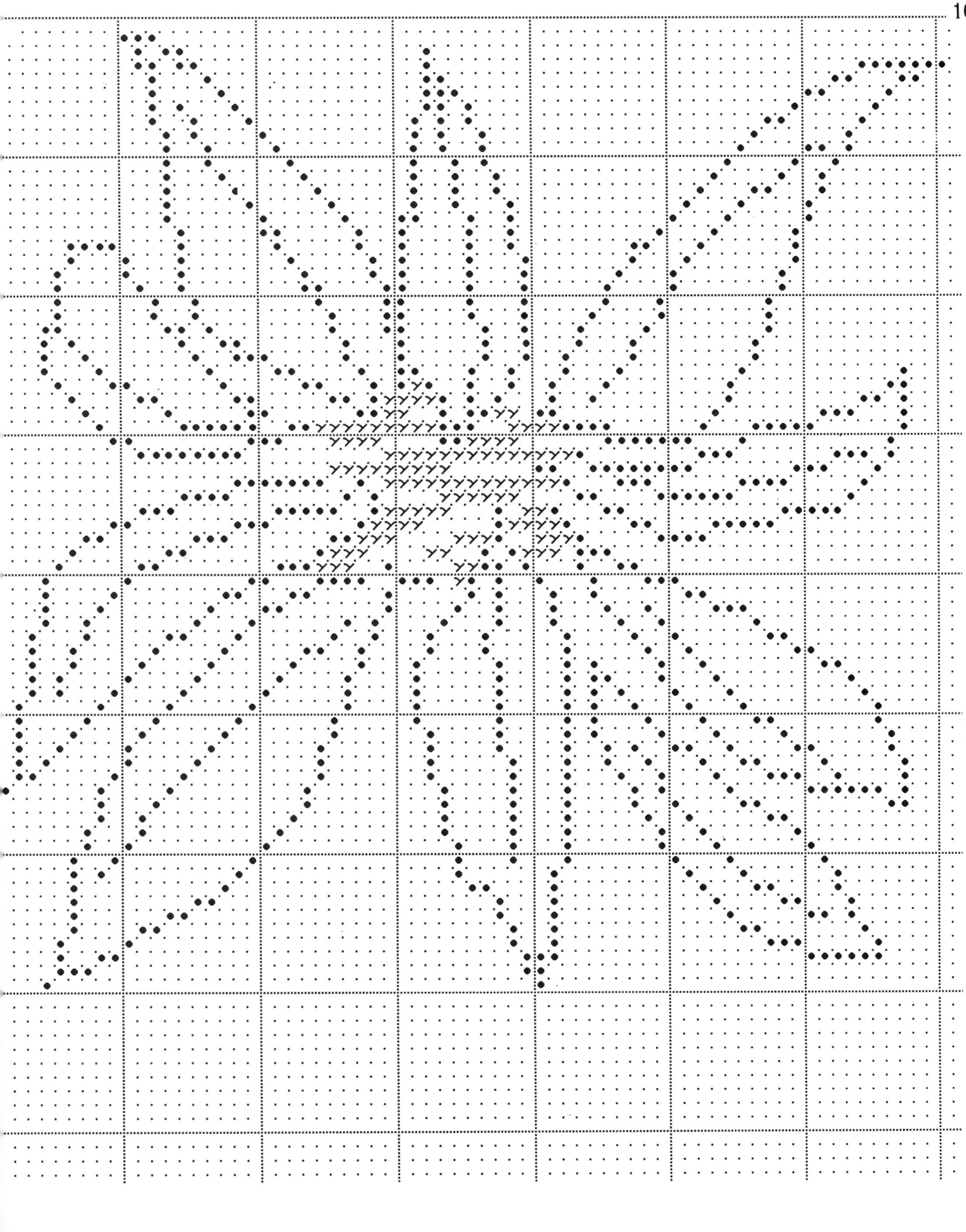

GIFTS TO MAKE

BABY'S COVERLET

● This reindeer coverlet is a unique and charming way to bring baby into the Christmas season. And don't forget to take snapshots! In years to come, you will treasure happy memories of baby tucked safe and sound under this coverlet.

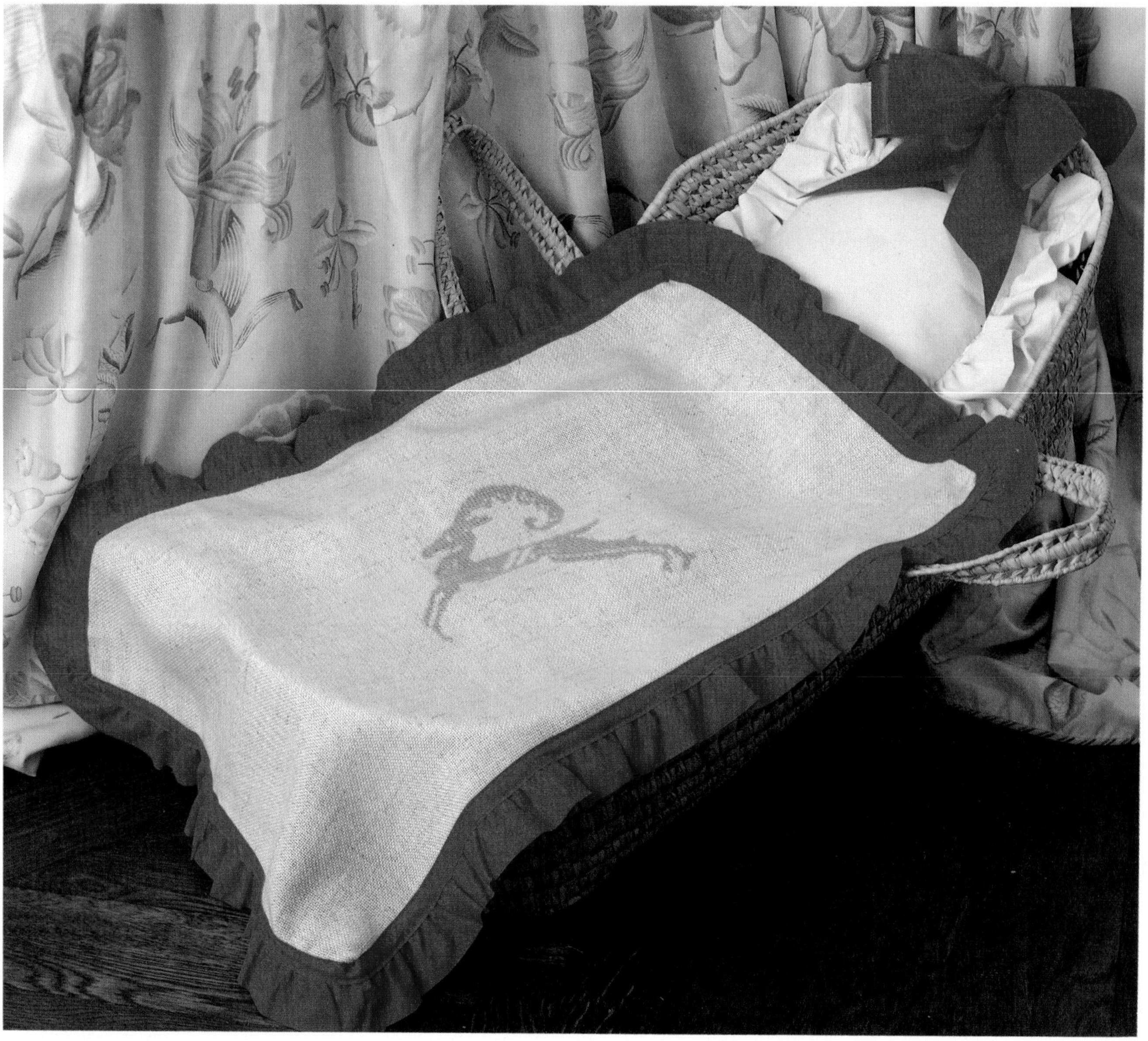

BABY'S COVERLET

Cut size: 32″ × 24″
Finished size: 28″ × 20″

#18 even-weave wool or cotton
4 strands of floss

DMC#
▼▼▼▼▼ 783 gold ochre

PIGS AND HEARTS TRAY HOLDER

● Tray holders are used in almost all Scandinavian homes at Christmas time. It's a decorative and functional way to keep much-used trays at hand.

The patterns are repeated, which means you can make the tray holder any length. We backed ours with a closely-woven fabric held with ornamental rings. These rings can be purchased at most needlework stores.

PIGS AND HEARTS TRAY HOLDE

Cut size: each strip 25″ × 7″
Finished size: each strip 21″ × 3″

#18 even-weave linen
 4 strands of floss

DMC#
●●●●● 349 red

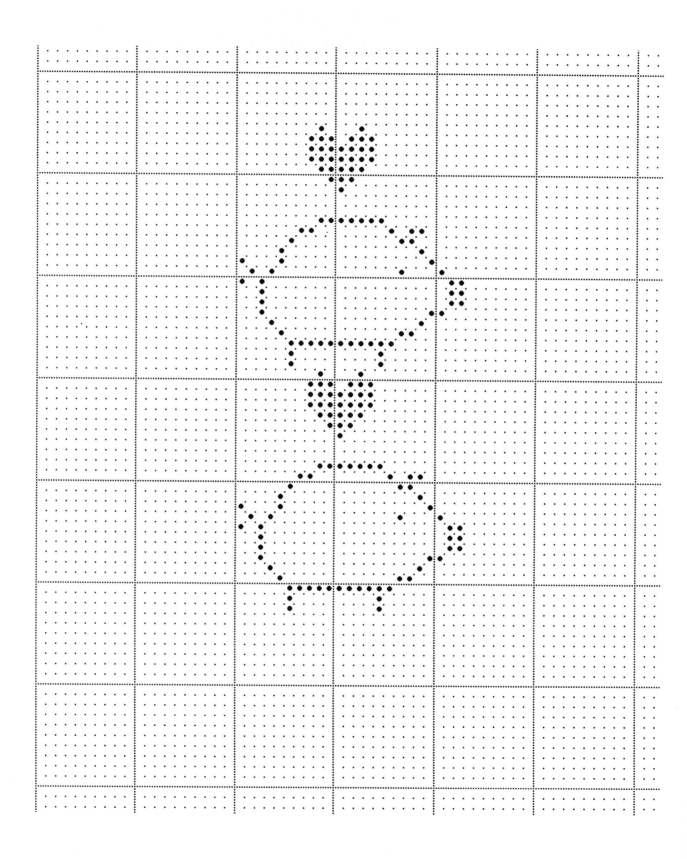

175

APPLE TRAY HOLDER

● This time *we* have the traditional Scandinavian tray holder, with an apple motif. Repeat the pattern until the tray holder is the desired length, then back each piece with closely woven fabric and attach to ornamental rings.

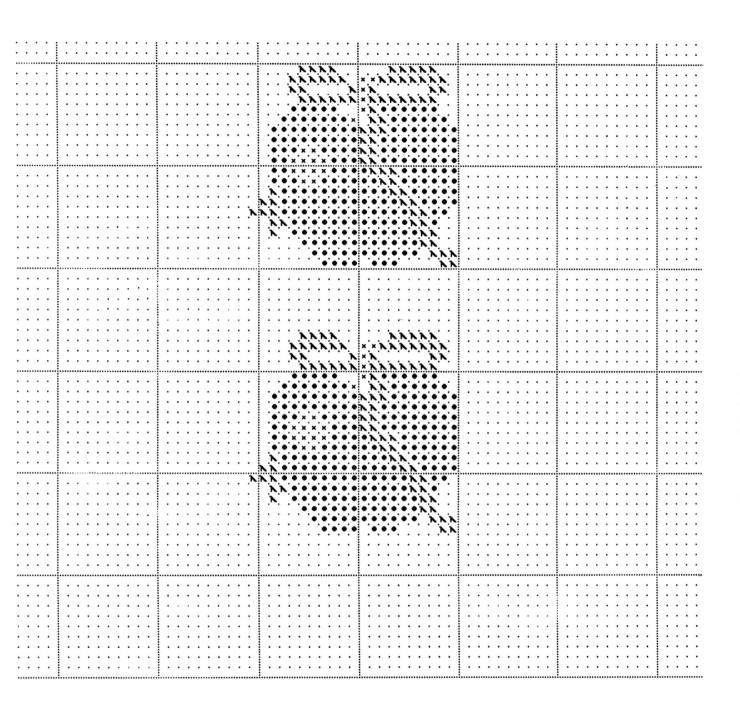

APPLE TRAY HOLDER

DMC#
- ●●● 349 red
- x x x   silver metallic
- ʌʌʌ 701 med. green

SANTA CHRISTMAS CARD

● *Make your own Christmas cards. What could be more personal? If you complete the cards and are enthusiastic about cross-stitching others, just flip through the book for other small motifs. You can use a design from an ornament, or the detail from a picture. Most needlework stores carry perforated paper cards in various sizes. This background is extremely suitable for cross-stitch.*

SANTA CHRISTMAS CARD

Cut size: 8″ × 8″
Finished size: 3″ × 3½″

#12 Aida cloth, or perforated paper
  3 strands of floss

	DMC#	
●●●●●	349	red
◇◇◇◇◇	948	flesh
✗✗✗✗✗	823	deep ultramarine blue
ᴌᴌᴌᴌᴌᴌ	989	med. olive
＋＋＋＋＋		white

STEEPLED-CHURCH CHRISTMAS CARD

● Here's another motif. A steepled-church Christmas card would be greatly appreciated by many people. Grandma would love getting one in the mail, and she'd probably frame it! There's no nicer way to say you care.

STEEPLED-CHURCH CHRISTMAS CARD

Cut size: 8″ × 8″
Finished size: 3″ × 3½″

#12 Aida cloth, or perforated paper
  3 strands of floss

	DMC#	
●●●●●●	349	red
⁄⁄⁄⁄⁄⁄	307	lt. yellow
٩٩٩٩٩٩	415	dove grey
×××××	823	dk. ultramarine blue
✧✧✧✧✧✧		gold metallic
■■■■■■	824	dk. blue
✦✦✦✦✦✦		white

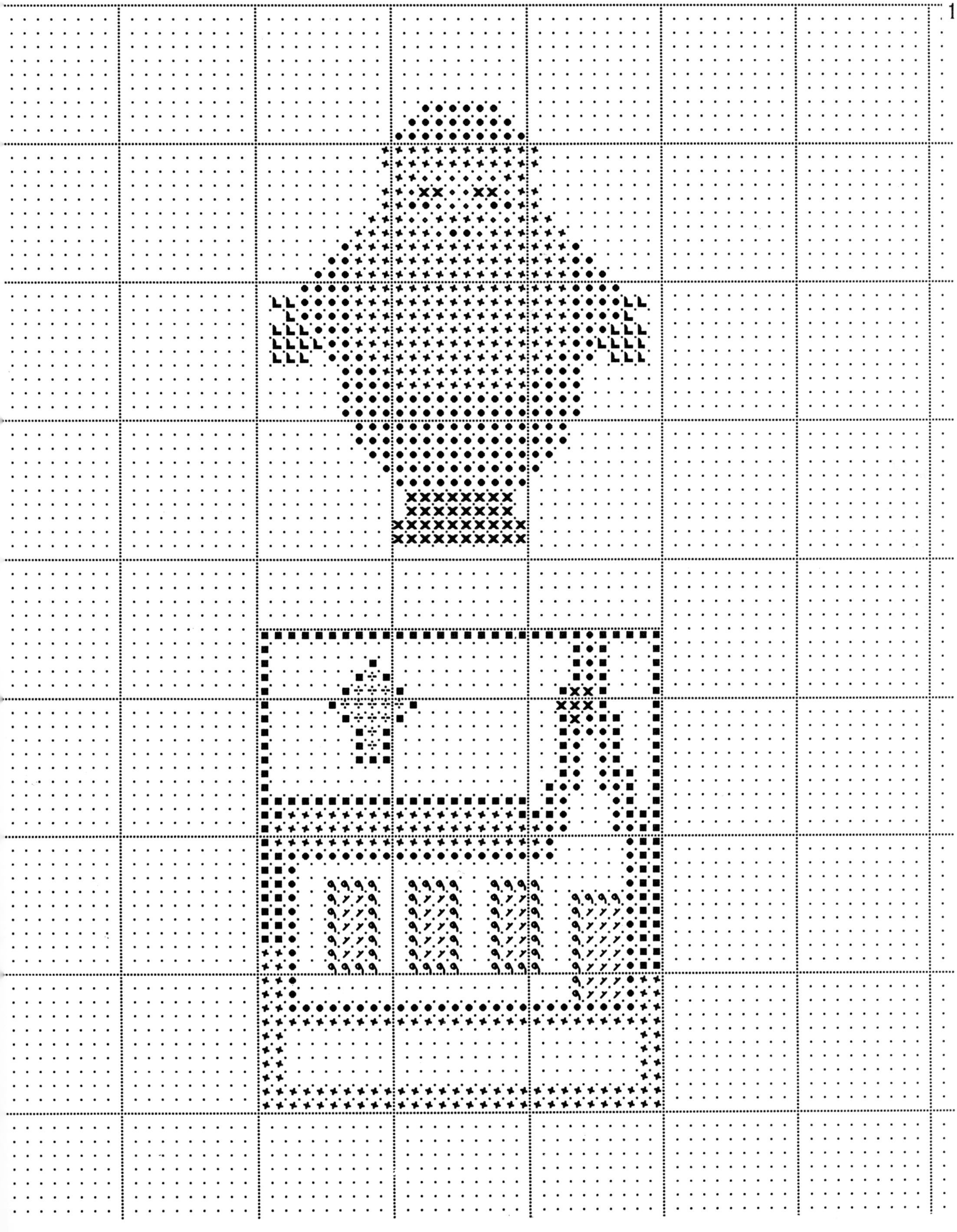

TEDDY BEAR GARLAND

• Use this bear chart and the Alphabet (see page 187) to create your garland. Teddy bears make everyone smile, and they'll look adorable wherever you hang them.

Our bears were stuffed with fiberfill to make them plump and happy.

TEDDY BEAR GARLAND

Cut size: 9″ × 10″
Finished size: 5½″ × 4½″

#12 Aida cloth
  3 strands of floss

	DMC#	
xxxxxx	823	deep ultramarine blue
ʟʟʟʟʟʟ	989	med. olive

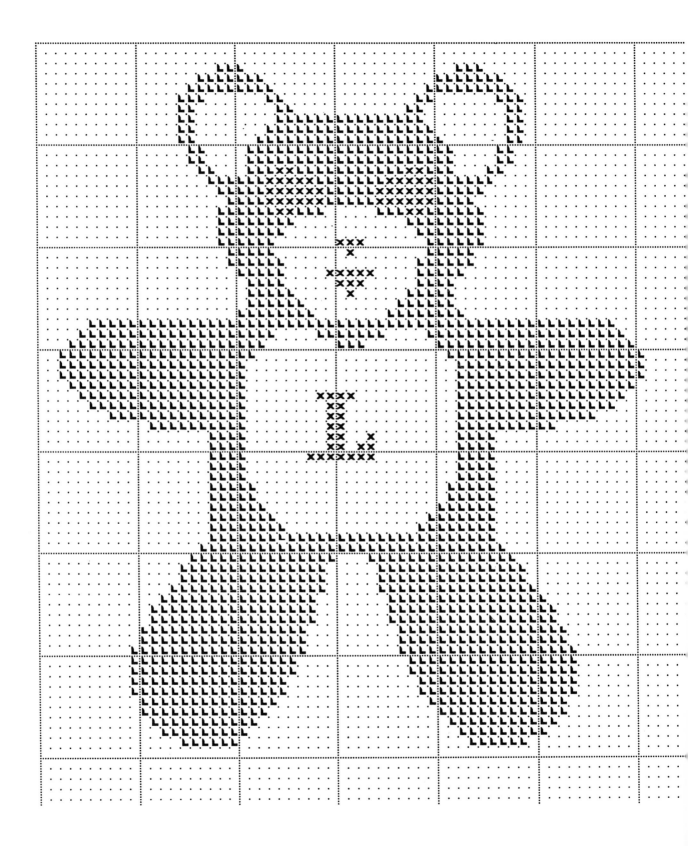

GNOMES
ALPHABET AND
NUMBERS

GNOMES ALPHABET

● *This alphabet was used throughout the book. We added a few merry gnomes for you to play with. Place them randomly around or next to a letter. Create your own cross-stitch mottoes or sayings, using the Gnomes Alphabet. Let them dance around and in between letters.*

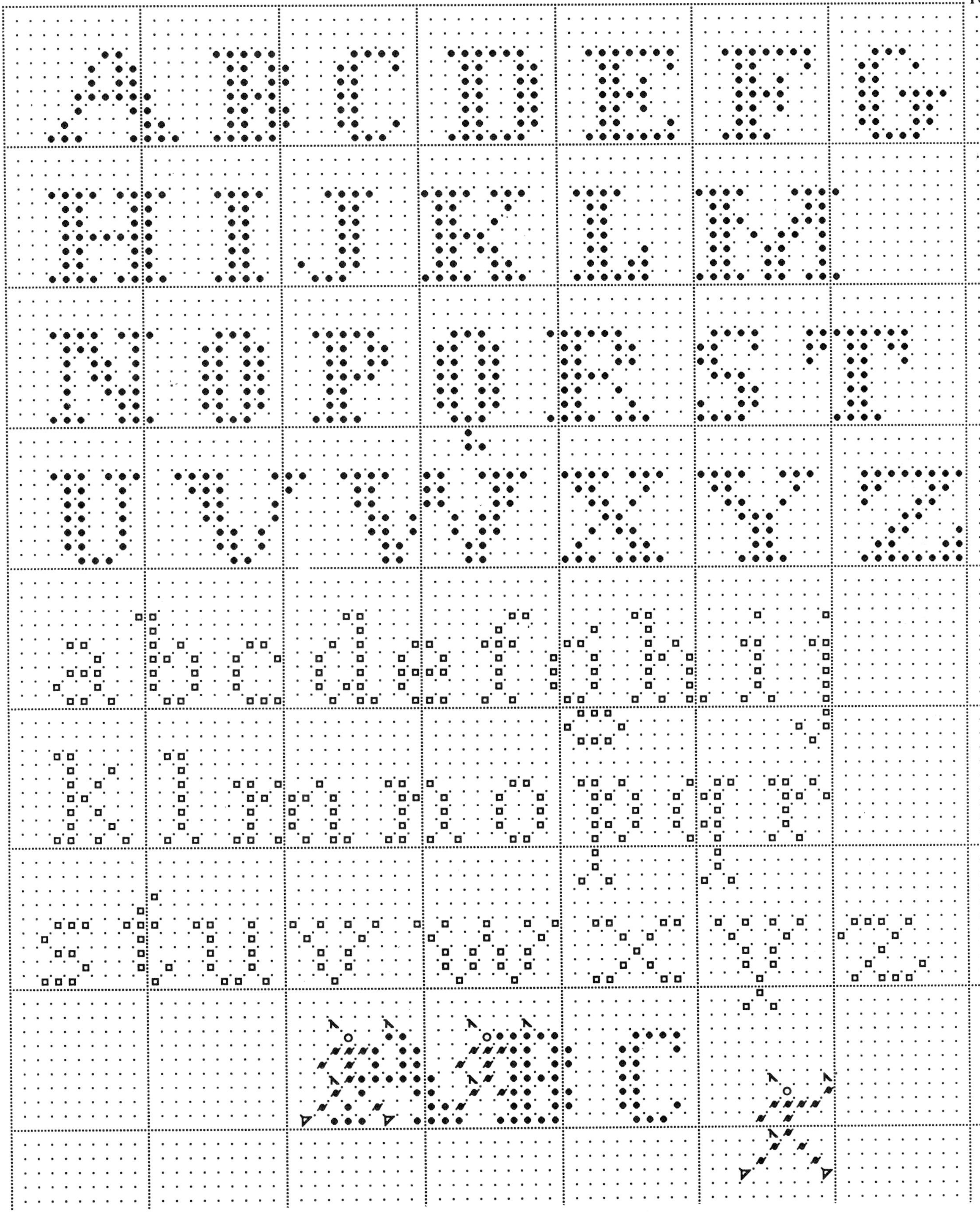

NUMBERS

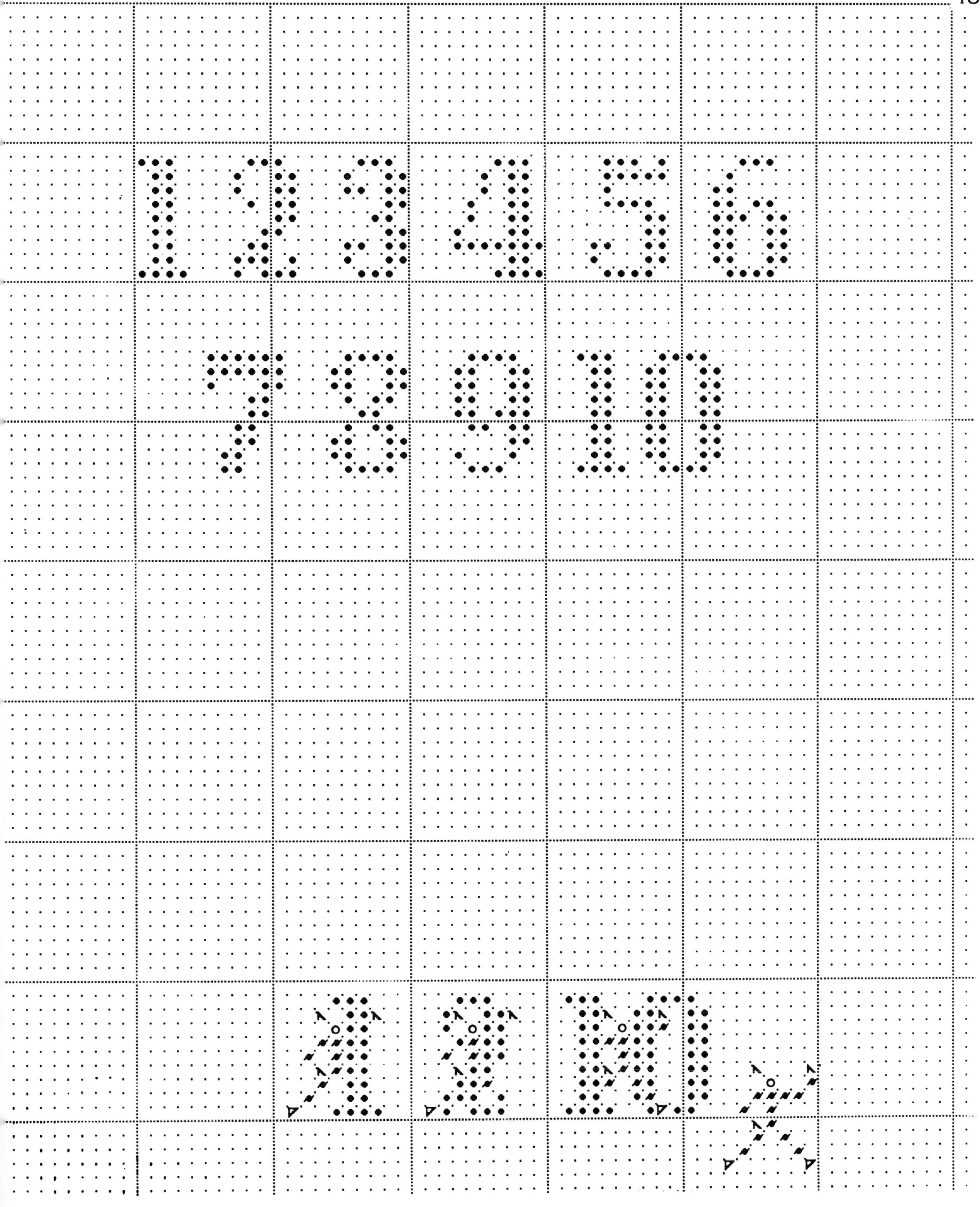

INDEX